THE RING OF FIRE

Polynesia's Sacred Isle

POLYNESIA'S
The Ring of Fire
VOLUME III

A Portrait of the South Sea island of Raiatea with Emphasis on the Traits that distinguish it from better-known neighbors such as Bora Bora and Tahiti, its traditional Myths and Legends and especially its Famous Flower, the *Tiare apetahi* that, in all the World, grows only on the Temehani, the Holy Mountain of Ancient Polynesia

SACRED ISLE

Edward Dodd

Illustrated with photographs, with drawings by Jacques Boullaire and Robert MacLean, and with reproductions of works by the early artists of Cook's voyages and Paul Gauguin

DODD, MEAD & COMPANY · NEW YORK

Printed in the United States of America

Library of Congress Cataloging in Publication Data

Dodd, Edward Howard, date
Polynesia's sacred isle.

(The Ring of fire ; v. 3)
Includes index.
1. Raiatea—Description and travel. 2. Folk-lore —Raiatea. 3. Apetahia raiateensis. 4. Dodd, Edward Howard, date I. Title.
DU870.D55 919.6'21 75-26513
ISBN 0-396-07227-5

The frontispiece-titlepage is a wash-drawing elevation of Raiatea by Henry Roberts who, Captain Gore (in command at the end of the third voyage, after Cook's death) says, "was principal assistant Hydrographer to Capt: Cook and is most certainly a verry Deserving young Man."

Henry Roberts, age 15, signed on the second voyage in 1771 as a midshipman. On the third he became Master's mate to the peppery William Bligh who was his junior at the time. He evidently had an inborn talent for drawing and chartwork as well as a personality that made friends of all his shipmates—a rare attainment amongst two such diverse groups under such long, enforced intimacy. His journal is most valuable and is illustrated, according to Beaglehole, with "charming wash drawings." He drafted the official General Chart of the third voyage, went on later to a naval command of his own and died in the West Indies at the age of 39.

for
Lisa, Roxana, and Ted

Acknowledgments

Throughout the text I have tried to acknowledge sources as I have quoted them or attributed passages and ideas. When you have been soaking yourself for as long as I have (for the past twenty years) in the whole field of Polynesian culture, it is impossible to give selective credit wherever it is due and since this is not an anthropological treatise, I have not presumed to the professional practice of specifying books, papers, or personal communication with page references, but have assumed instead that any one interested in challenging me or in seeking further detail, would be sufficiently cognizant of the author involved to find what he wants. They are all familiar enough to any specialist and C. R. H. Taylor's magnificent PACIFIC BIBLIOGRAPHY will easily point the way to any newcomer. But in addition to sources acknowledged in the text, I owe special thanks to the advice, suggestion, and wisdom of a few friends who have helped most kindly even though, in some cases, they may not have realized they were doing so, and are thus clearly exonerated from any blame for unpalatable opinions, bias, or just plain errors of any sort.

For the essential substance of the book I owe much to Kenneth Emory, Bengt Danielsson, Gladys and Medford Kellum, Aurora Natua, and Turo Haapa, and a grateful bow to Dr. Harold St. John for his rare-to-come-by guidance on the tiare apetahi.

For imaginative suggestions in library research Dr. Charles Long and Diane Schwartz of the New York Botanical, Margaret Titcomb (as usual) of the Bishop Museum, and especially Edward Connery Lathem, Librarian of Dartmouth College, not only for his endless facilities, but most of all for his careful and brilliant suggestions in reading the manuscript.

For photography, firstly Axel Poignant of London and again to Kenneth Emory and warmly to Michel Liaut of Raiatea who climbed the mountain especially to photograph the great Hole for me.

For drawings, the lovely, essential Polynesia of Jacques Boullaire and the adroit expository art of Robert MacLean.

For patience and precision in production, Helen Winfield and Martha Schwerin.

Contents

Raiatea! Raiatea nei!
Raiatea fenua here no toe mau tamarii
Raiatea rupe rupe
Raiatea fenua here no toe mau tamarii
Fenua herehia no toe mau tamarii
I Raiatea nei!
E hau maru e maru
To oe rai e topa
Ra te mahana
I Raiatea nei!

Raiatea! Raiatea behold!
Raiatea, cherished land for all thy children
Raiatea flourishing, beautiful
Raiatea land beloved for thine offspring
Land cherished for all thy sons
In Raiatea here!
A peaceful realm
Your sky is enchanting
When the sun goes down
O Raiatea!

CHAPTER ONE

A Present-Day Landfall

This is a book about an island, a very small island in the center of the Pacific Ocean, almost exactly in the center, with no continental land within 3000 miles in any direction around the great ocean's rim; a rim which is sometimes called "the ring of fire" because of the many volcanoes and the earthquake faults that run from the coast of Chile by way of California to Alaska, arch over the far north, through the Aleutian Islands to Japan, bend southward, occasionally shattering parts of New Guinea, dive under sea into the great Tongan submarine trench, and thence plunge still further south, to leave plumes of smoke flowing from the mountains of New Zealand. But the book is not only about the island, it is also about the culture of the Polynesian race, and about the men and women who inhabit all of the thousands of islands which lie within the huge ocean bowl that is encompassed by the ring of fire. It speculates on the geological origins of this volcanic island and its neighbors. There is a good deal about the *tiare apetahi*, the lovely flower that grows only on this island, and the theories that try to account for such a strange botanical occurrence. Many other South Sea curiosities connected with the island are related, but mainly the book concerns itself with the people, their legends, superstitions, customs, religious beliefs, and history.

Since our particular island, Raiatea, is only some twenty miles long and ten or twelve wide, it may seem an almost neglegible piece of land on which to base the tale of a human culture, one that, though small in population, is more widely distributed than any other in the world. But the point is that this little island was, I believe, the birthplace of the ultimate flowering of that culture. From its original genes, the race as we have known it since its discovery by Europeans, developed and eventually matured. So, starting here is perhaps no more illogical than starting a description of the Christian culture in tiny Palestine. Besides this book does not attempt to cover the breadth and depth of Polynesian culture, it only gathers together the scraps and hints and insights that are left to us from chants and recitations long gone by, oral traditions of a race that never set pen to paper, whose only tangible bequests are its sculpture, its artifacts, its fleshly descendants and their own individual ways. Nor in attempting to recreate this culture will we pay much attention to its practical workings or its warlike doings. This narrative may be said to be a revelation or reminiscence of an affair—yes, a love affair, with an island. So you must not expect dispassionate evaluations, nor statistics, nor cool judgments. No, this is a personal approach such as would appeal more to a romantic than to an historian or to an objective anthropologist.

Raiatea was the "holy land" of ancient Polynesia. Its original name was Havai'i or Havaiki. (How that *k* came to be dropped out and how many other letters came to be interchanged, and some of the mysteries of the glottal stop are explained in the Appendix at the end of the book.)

But before launching upon our main speculations on the origins of Raiatea and the pre-European ways of its ancient people, let me sketch briefly the background of our personal, present-day involvement with the island.

It was a full forty years gone by when I first visited Raiatea. Five of us, graduates of the class of 1928 at Yale, had joined together to buy a schooner and "sail around the world." (Actually it was our parents who bought the schooner and none of us sailed all the way around the world. But the schooner *Chance* with some changes in crew did make the whole course and most of us made the whole Pacific).

When we dropped anchor in the copious and secure harbor of Uturoa a few miles north of Opoa where Cook had moored the *Endeavour* one hundred and sixty years before us, we rowed ashore to a small village which was largely populated by Chinese. We spent the night ashore in a rickety little hotel called the "Hinano." I remember

The schooner *Chance* was built in Lunenberg, Nova Scotia, from the yard and model of a "Bluenose" shipwright, so she was more of a fisherman than a yacht, as comfortable and seaworthy as a sailing vessel could be. She was 76 feet overall, large enough to accommodate seven or eight, but when only five of us worked her from Fiji to Sydney, we found that number the best fit of all.

well that on that first night and for many nights thereafter my sleeping companion was a fragrant little Polynesian girl, named Nui, and I say sleeping companion advisedly because although we bedded together for several weeks with great congeniality and pleasure she always remained a virgin. Those were peaceful leisurely days in Raiatea after the very active life of Tahiti. We had brought a Frenchman with us for the short overnight sail from Paea. He was a journalist and since he had a mechanical turn of mind we took advantage of him and his good nature to dismantle our engine and replace a faulty main gasket. Tom, our engineer, was of course in charge. He could speak no French and the journalist no English. So I, who could speak no mechanics acted as interpreter. I learned a good deal in that dark, sweaty engine hold, how, for instance to translate a monkey wrench into French and nuts and bolts, pistons, valves and petcocks. But somehow we did manage to take the beast apart and to put it together again so that it operated a bit better than it had before.

Once it was running again I suppose we must have felt compelled to use it, for we decided to run right around the island. We took the resident medical staff, a Dr. Bizien and his wife and had a gala few days cruising the reef-locked lagoon of Raiatea.

Turia

At the southern end of the island we anchored for a night at Fetuna. And there we went ashore and walked in the moonlight. It was a charming drowsy little village, cut off entirely from the rest of the island for the road did not come halfway down on either side. Fetuna could be reached only by boat. To be sure the little island steamer came from Uturoa every week or perhaps every two weeks, or if the turtles were running at Maupiti, once a month. But the settlement had two faded-blue Chinese stores and a bakery, so it was comfortably self-sufficient especially since its lagoon was always swarming with fish and its valleys were crowded with coco palms, breadfruit, and bananas. With its wide harbor and deep-blue pass through the reef and past the islet of Nao Nao, Fetuna became my South Sea idyll. Thirty years later when I took my wife Camille there, it had lost nothing of its magic. At that time in the late 1950's we were just entering our Polynesian researches and were becoming acquainted with the islands and their people. We had hired a little outboard for the day from Ah Hin who was the principal

Looking down from the hill above our house upon the islet or *motu* of Nao Nao and to the left of it the deep water pass through the reef into the harbor of Fetuna. *Nao Nao* means many, many mosquitoes and they were indeed thick upon the island, but they rarely came across the lagoon to bother us.

Opposite
Fetuna in 1929. This photograph taken by my shipmate Alexander Brown looks south along the shore where we met Turo, to the point where we finally built our house. If you took a picture from the same location today, you would find that only the coconut trees had changed and they don't change much.

power and factotum of the town of Uturoa. His home was the erstwhile Hinano Hotel where I first lay with Nui and he now managed a new Hinano, a much more extensive establishment; a cement-block facility with rooms and toilets upstairs and a pool room, bar and restaurant below. There my wife and I stayed when we first came to the island until Ah Hin managed to find for us a little cottage two or three miles below Uturoa out of sound and sight of that bustling metropolis.

The day Ah Hin took us around the island in his outboard, we stopped at Fetuna for lunch. Afterward I took Camille for a walk along the curving footpath to the southernmost tip of the island. It was exactly as I remembered it thirty-odd years before, indeed startingly so—the purau trees, hibiscus, and oleanders arching over to form an alleyway spangled with red and yellow flowers, with glimpses of the blue-green lagoon on the left, and upward-sweeping, yellow-green hills on the right. We thought. This is the place for us! If only we could find a point of land and built a bamboo house.

Just then a young man came toward us on a bicycle. We stepped aside to let him pass, but he slowed to a stop and greeted us. He spoke good French, which is unusual in Fetuna, and he walked along with us toward the point. We soon found ourselves getting along most congenially and presently we shared with him our fanciful notion of acquiring a small piece of land and building a house. He said it might be difficult, for the natives never want to part with their land and the French would permit only Frenchmen to settle, but he suggested that we come back in a few days and stay at his father's house. He would do some inquiring in the meantime and we could explore any possibilities together. It seemed an impulsive invitation, and we were reluctant to impose ourselves, but impulses seemed to be running our way in Fetuna and the Polynesians are impulsive people. It was past time for us to leave, but our new friend walked back to the wharf with us and we made a date to return, this time on the island boat that makes its weekly way from Uturoa.

The name of the boy we met on that footpath is Turo, and over the years since 1961 when we first met he has

Farika paring purau shoots and Turo cutting up a lobster.

become a son to us, his wife our daughter, and their seven children our grandchildren. After our first night's visit to his father's house, where he regaled us with beautiful lobsters fresh from their bay and where we became acquainted with Turo's wife, Farika, (there was only one baby then, little Noeline), and his parents, we set about our mission. We would stroll along the shore and pick out a likely spot. Turo would inquire here and there, and invariably come back with a negative; "aita." Almost all Polynesian land is owned by families. Sometimes as many as 30 or 40 people will have, or will claim, an ownership interest in only a few hectares, and there were always some of them who had intended to build someday on exactly the spot we had chosen. Also, there were always others, distant aunts, uncles, or cousins who were away in Tahiti and could not be consulted.

So it went, intermittently, over a couple of years until one of Turo's grandmothers (adoptive, but very close) gave him permission to build a "remblai" out into the lagoon on her land and a house on it. A remblai is a landfill protuberance or extension. Retaining walls of coral heads are first constructed in the lagoon, from the sloping beach out to a depth of two or more feet, these heads rising about three feet above the surface of the water. The coral battlements against the sea have to be very strong, some three or four feet thick. The area enclosed by them is next filled with more loose coral, rubble, and sand, and finally, with a good thick layer of good, rich earth from the hills.

I wanted to build a graceful, curving bulge into the lagoon, but the French authorities would have none of that. It must be rectangular. Why? Réglements! So we decided on a square, 20 meters by 20 meters, generous enough to allow for a nice garden in the back and a small turtle-and-fish enclosure in one corner. I designed an old-time Raiatean house; that is, one with the traditional rounded ends. And one year while we were in Europe poring through museums in search of pictures, tracing provenances, and seeking permissions for our book on Polynesian art, Turo and his grandfather, Puna'auia, the carpenter, built the house. They did not pay much attention to my interior layout, but on the outside it turned out

Our little house at Fetuna seen from the dock that runs out over the shoal coral to the sudden deep blue of the lagoon. The "notch" in the remblai at the left was later fenced to contain sea turtles.

Turo's father, Narii, with a bunch of *fei*, the mountain plantain which, unlike the banana, must be cooked and has always been one of the favorite staple foods of the Raiateans.

to be a beauty, and is always admired nostalgically by anyone at all acquainted with prehistoric Polynesia.

Our practical arrangements were simple and clearly understood. We Dodds paid all costs of construction. Turo's grandmother owned the newly created land, granting us a nine-year lease in return for repossession of it after that time. Turo owned the house on the same basis, except it was agreed that when Camille and I chose to occupy it, he and his family would move elsewhere, to reoccupy when we had left. We typed up a short memo about this, in duplicate, and several of us signed the document, but I'm sure no one has ever looked at it since, nor very probably will anyone ever do so, for no doubt by now both copies are lost. I know mine is.

It has been our house for some eleven years now, and never has there been the slightest friction between the Tehiotaata family and ourselves. Tehiotaata means the Essence of Man. Turo's father, Narii, has now been chief of the district of Fetuna for some six or seven years. He is a splendid man, but since he cannot read or write, and speaks only Tahitian, Turo has to handle all paperwork (and in French colonies there is plenty), also much translation with the Administrateur in Uturoa, the doctors, dentists, schoolteachers, and police, all of whom keep a stern eye on their native subjects, and make a very genial living for themselves in doing so.

The view from the window where we work by day, with Oropiro, the "evil" mountain that dominates our whole Fetuna area, rising to the left and falling off at the great rock, Haapapara, which looks like a precipice above the flat land of the point extending into the lagoon.

That, then, is how we came to Fetuna. We have returned every couple of years for two, three, or four months at a time, not only escaping Vermont winters, but also working into finished books the mass of materials we had collected in our travels to museums in Europe, America, Hawaii, New Zealand (even as far abroad as Madagascar and Easter Island) and researching in the principal libraries of the world possessing good Polynesian collections, and associating with anthropologists, archaeologists, and Polynesian specialists. It has always been a peaceful place, Fetuna, away from telephones and terrestrial transport, no electricity to light our books or my pencil or Camille's typewriter at night, but plenty of bright sunshine to light them by day.

The books on Polynesian art and Polynesian seafaring have long since been published, and now we have completed this third book, on Polynesian culture, stemming from its core in Raiatea. A great deal has been written about this culture from the viewpoints of Tahiti, Hawaii, New Zealand and Easter, very little from the viewpoints of the Marquesas, or the Cooks and Australs. The multitude of writers bemused by Tahiti always consider Raiatea a province or appendage. Actually it is Hawaiki, the homeland, and Tahiti is "the fish that swam away." Raiatea is considerably smaller and to a present-day tourist or to an erstwhile visitor, like Pierre Loti or Gauguin or Rupert Brooke, merely an outlying, primitive terra incognita of the glamorous Cythere of Bougainville (or Paris of the Pacific, as it is widely known today). But Raiatea has its own charms, and it has its deep significances too, reaching way back into the origins of the Polynesian peoples before its offspring, Tahiti, stole the limelight of the *popa'a*, the *papa langi* or sky breakers, who came from the world beyond the great ocean.

The same view at night with the moon rising in the east and a bonfire of coconut husks still burning on the shore below. Oropiro is the *oro* (mountain) *piro* (foul or evil) because from him come the sudden violent storms that lash fishing canoes returning from the reef and tear thatch from houses.

CHAPTER TWO

Quest for the Flower

Shall we start with the flower? Surely it is unique, the only one of its kind in the whole world. Surely it is beautiful too. Moreover, it has a spiritual tradition that links, in a way, the much older geology and botany of the island with the much younger inhabitant of it, Polynesian man.

Traditionally, and long before the arrival of Europeans in the Pacific, the flower is said to have been called the "tiare apetahi." In Tahitian the translation of "tiare" is, according to present-day usage and present-day dictionaries, simply flower. Even in the earliest dictionary we have (ostensibly that of the missionary John Davies, later assisted by his confrere D. Darling, compiled in the 1820's though not published until 1851), tiare means "flowers or blossoms in general." Any flower nowadays is a tiare, but as we shall see presently this may not always have been so. "Apetahi" is more complex. Apetahi is listed by Davies as "to look aside, or askance." The most noticeable characteristic of the tiare apetahi is the deep fissure that splits it. It might, therefore, be called a one-sided flower, and there may thus be some relation of meaning. A Tahitian friend of mine who is dedicated to the old ways and who is knowledgeable of them as well, says that the word "Ape" was said to describe how a stranger or a suspicious man would shift his eyes from side to side, ever wary, as he walked through a crowd of strangers or potential enemies, searching out a friend in the gathering, making also a quick toss of the cheek, as if to avoid a slap. The flower hardly does that, but the second part of its name, "tahi," means one, or one-sided; therefore a half-flower. And it does in a way "ride side-saddle" when worn behind the ear, as no other flower can do. Some years after learning

Opposite
The tiare apetahi with its large buds nestling in the leaves of its bushes, 2000 feet high on a shoulder of the Temehani.

this from my friend, I went browsing again in Davies, to see what he wrote separately about the two parts of the word. Ape, he says, means "the act of flinching from danger or avoiding the consequence of an argument." Then I chanced to look back a little in his book and came upon ap*a*tahi: "to cast a side glance at a person on account of displeasure or of shame." And a second meaning: "one sided, as a certain flower is said to be, tiare apatahi: see tiare." But when one turns to tiare one finds merely "the name of a sweet scented flower" and "flowers or blossoms in general." His only pertinent definition of tahi is "a one in counting." Since this dictionary was compiled from information supplied by several of the missionaries, it seems natural enough that spellings and meanings should vary a bit.

Botanists object to the word tiare as applied to this particular flower because the best known tiare in the islands is the tiare Tahiti (or tiare Taiti, as it is commonly called), which is clearly a gardenia which the apetahi is clearly not. So, they have named it "*Apetahia raiateensis*," (capitalizing the genus and italicizing both genus and species as is the established botanical method). At least they have had the graciousness to preserve, perhaps to immortalize, its indigenous surname, rather than to call it after its first European discoverer, as was (and still is) the prevalent Linnean custom. Let us be thankful therefore that it is not *Banksia raiateensis*, not *Vancouveria*, nor *Smithia*, nor *Jonesia*. All this may seem to be botanical quibbling, but it may have sturdy historical grounding also. The Polynesian's botanical knowledge has been widely recognized and admired from earliest times. There was never any confusion of his names for any living thing.

The first mention of our flower that I have been able to trace occurs in Sidney Parkinson's *Journal*, and can be dated in late July of 1769, when Cook's *Endeavour* first visited and, as the European is wont to say, "discovered" the island. Parkinson was chief artist of Cook's first expedition. In his *Journal* he prints a list of "Plants of Ufe for Food, Medicine &c in Otaheite," 83 of them, with their native names in all cases and their Latin names in all but 11 cases. "E apatahei. An elegant flower which I alfo did

Opposite
Sydney Parkinson's painting of the tiare tahiti, reproduced from the original in the lovely collection at the British Museum of Natural History.

The number of petals on this flower varies greatly, from four or five to as many as eleven. Often the petal numbers differ even among flowers on the same bush. Six, seven, and eight are the most common and seven-petaled flowers are the lucky ones —first choice to wear behind your ear.

The tiare apetahi in contrast always has five petals and five only.

Parkinson's complete list of plants of use for food, medicine, and so forth, will be found in the Appendix

not see" is no. 79 on the list and has no Latin name. Indeed our flower did not acquire one until a hundred and thirteen years later, in 1882, when the French botanist H. Baillon first "published" it in a *Bulletin* of the Société Linnéenne de Paris. Meanwhile, it had apparently gained a reputation of some prominence amongst botanists. Speci-

Opposite
Although H. Baillon was the first botanist to describe and classify the tiare apetahi in 1882, another French botanist, Emmanuel Drake del Castillo, was the first to draw a picture of it and publish it in his "Illustrationes Florae Insularum Maris Pacifici," dated, on the title page, 1886, but actually issued in parts over a period between 1886 and 1892. It seems appropriate that such a rare and exquisite flower should be introduced visually to the botanical world by such a pleasant drawing and by an artist with such an aura of glamour. Drake del Castillo had an English grandfather named Drake, who settled in Cuba and married a Spanish lady of high family and fortune named del Castillo. Their son moved to Paris, where Emmanuel was born in 1855. Both of his parents died when he was young, so this grandson of an English island in the North Sea and of a Spanish island in the Caribbean became a native of France who devoted his life to the study of the flora of the French islands of the Pacific Ocean and of Madagascar in the Indian Ocean.

According to the illustrious master of his botanical studies, Emmanuel was a quiet, modest man of brilliant intellect and life-long dedication to science. His very considerable wealth founded one of the finest herbaria and botanical libraries in France, and although his curious Anglo-Hispanic name makes him hard to locate in our library catalogs, he shall always be revered (by this writer at least) for his superb rendering of the shy apetahi, shown here life size.

mens were collected and attempts to grow them elsewhere were made. But the apetahi refused to flourish anywhere except on its own mountain slopes, on its own little island in the middle of the Pacific. Even today, when transported by helicopter to the same altitudes in nearby Tahiti, it has refused to take root. It has become one of the most famous recluses of the botanical world, and to see it you must climb its mountain and meet it on its own exclusive homesite. That is what Camille and I did, as shall be recounted later, but let me first wind up my investigation of the flower's native name, tiare.

As I have said, tiare is the name in the Tahitian language used to designate any flower, and I had long thought we might gently accuse the botanists of being a bit snobbish in rejecting it. Then, as I looked more closely at Parkinson's list, I saw number 8: "E teea—ree *Gardenia florida.* This was originally brought from fome other ifland to Otaheite, and there planted on account of its moft fragrant flower, which they crop as foon as grown and ftick in their ears, calling it E teea-ree, that is, the flower, by way of eminence." No other of his 83 is listed as a tiare. (For those who may not be familiar with the Tahitian's way of expressing himself, it might be well to point out here that he used and still uses many expletives or prefixes. Cook did not realize, when he first heard the natives name their island, that in saying Otahiti, they meant O (that is) Tahiti. E (pronounced *ay*) or Te means much the same sort of thing, though it is closer to our article the. We call our flower's mountain the Temehani, and in doing so we are in effect saying the the Mehani. But the Polynesian is not fussy about things like this, and, being Frenchified, is perfectly happy to point out to you le Temehani. Davies lists "Mehani, the name of a mountain in Raiatea, where the ghosts of the dead were said to go.")

And that brings us to another aspect of this flower, the spiritual or supernatural. But before exploring this most vital and fascinating facet, let us go back to Parkinson and try to tidy up that odd ending of his reference to the tiare, *Gardenia florida*, "the flower by way of eminence." Some writers have speculated that tiare is an elision of the two words Te-arii. The arii in Tahiti were the high-born chiefs,

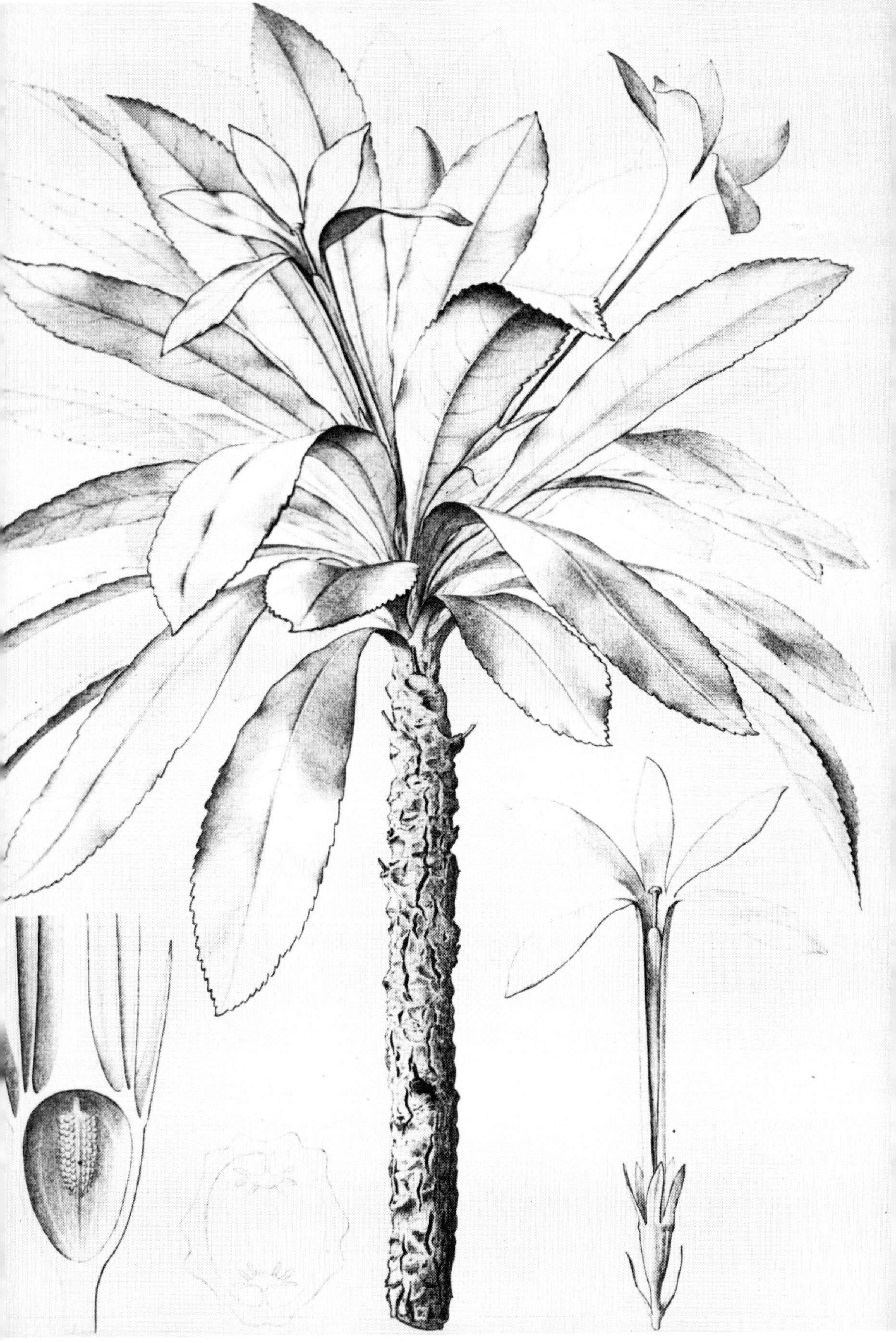

From the point of view of an oldtime Raiatean, could it be that the flower was given a name that denoted fear of a slap on the cheek in order to warn the lowborn to be wary of it?

the princes of the realm. Perhaps the gardenia was named for them, but just to demonstrate how things can get mixed around in Polynesia, there is no evidence that the tiare taiti was sacred to the nobility. There is, on the other hand, a firm tradition that the tiare apetahi of Raiatea was reserved exclusively for the use of the "royalty" of the island. An old story says that the tiare apetahi represented the five fingers of the hand of a Tahitian princess who was forbidden to marry her Raiatean lover. "Tau tiare apetahi oe" is an ancient poetic Raiatean term expressing the highest and most affectionate appreciation of a darling child or loved one. The French explorer, M. Vesco, who was the first white man to pick the flower, said the natives claimed that the reason it would never grow elsewhere was because it was reserved exclusively for the chiefs and queens of Raiatea.

That this flower was tapu in olden times is not surprising, because everything rare and precious, such as a turtle or a red-feather girdle or the eye of a sacrifical victim, was reserved for the delectation of the high chiefs and the taua. The high chiefs of Raiatea were the Tamatoa, who were the highest of all in the Society or Tahitian Islands. Although not nearly as large as Tahiti, it was to Raiatea the holy land; to the "international" marae of Taputapuatea at Opoa that chiefs were brought for investiture, even from as far away as Aotea, as New Zealand was called before Abel Tasman found it.

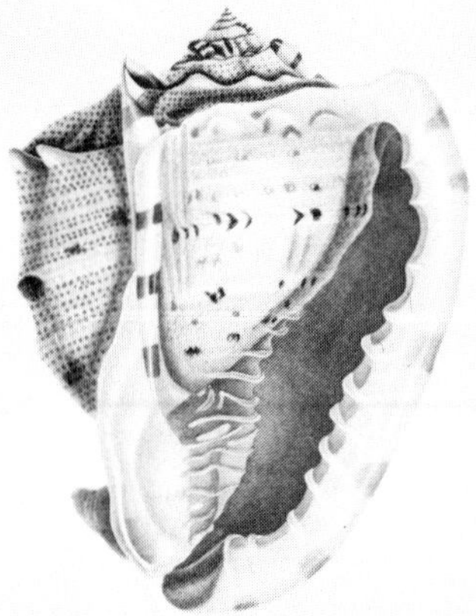

We started our climb with cautious hearts that sunny morning. Two years before we had set out confidently, even jauntily. The Temehani did not look high or steep, as mountains go. There were no rock faces or icy ridges. This would be easy enough, we had thought; long, undulating ridges, very little underbrush, no trees at all up on the heights. The tropic sun would make climbing hot, but we were used to it, and we thought we had plenty of time to walk slowly and to rest often. So we had scrambled along, up and down, down and up, until the ridges became endless and every time we surmounted one, we descended another, gaining a bit no doubt, a small percentage of altitude in every mile, but losing a little each time in our hearts and our hopes. And our feet did not improve as they slipped and slid over slimy clay or stumbled and twisted over stony brook beds. As the day wore on, we rested more and more often under the occasional clusters of maape trees, the Polynesian chestnuts, that provided cool shade more and more conveniently in small hollows along the way. That afternoon the sun sank with an unusual rapidity, and we had to be high up on the mountain where the flowers were before it set. Obviously, we could

A grove of *maape*, the Polynesian chestnut trees, whose weirdly weaving buttress roots and high, luscious crowns cast mysterious but cooling and comfortable shade for the walker on the hills.

not negotiate slippery ridges and rocky streams in the dark, and it was essential to be amongst the flowers at dawn when the rising sun would cause their buds to pop like little muted firecrackers. Then the petals would spring apart and split the flower down its side, so that it looked like half a flower instead of a whole one.

When a particularly steep ridge came up you had to go down on hands and toes, slinging your pack or basket or bundle along your back as best you could. At the crest of one of these ridges there rose a conical tower of rock, straight up it seemed and surely unclimbable. But the two boys who were our "guides" scampered up and around it as if it were a circular staircase on the outside of a lighthouse. The only trouble was that there were no stairs or steps that we could see, just little extrusions of rock no bigger than half loaves of bread, projecting occasionally and with a most inconsiderate irregularity of spacing. Tufts of coarse grass to swing on thrust themselves out obligingly, but one dared not put much weight on them. About halfway up the tower there was to be sure a flattish slope, somewhat like a twisted toboggan on a steep grade, onto which one could cast a trembling body and hitch it up convulsively to another succession of winding bread loaves. It all seemed quite impossible, but at last, there we were on the top, able to crawl panting to a flat space on a continuation of the ridge.

It took some time for us to breathe again regularly and to gain some modicum of composure. But this was lost promptly when we looked about us. The mountain fell away on all sides precipitately, a thousand feet or more. The prospect was beautiful. Bright, yellow-green hillsides swept down to the purple lagoon, across which the blue-green shoals of the reef spread to the foaming white lines of the breakers; beyond these stretched the dark blue ocean, seeming as still as a bathtub at this height, but rolling with great swells had you been upon it. Occasionally little, palm-studded islets punctuated the reef and marked the open, bluewater passes through the coral barrier. Yes, it was beautiful, surpassingly so, but it was also frightening, because one little slip on the side of that turret of rock on which we were crouching would have sent us rocketing down those glistening green slopes, bleeding, bruised and dead, into the blue lagoon. But then we realized that, of course all these palpitations were our own fault, not the mountain's. We were elderly, all three of us; our Tahitian friend, Aurora, and ourselves. Camille had a bothersome ankle from a bicycle fall. (In San Francisco, on the way back, it turned out to have been broken or at least cracked). Most of all we were not mountain climbers; we did not relish heights, and we never expected even this brief one on the vast undulating Temehani.

There was nowhere else to go but up, up that next ridge. The climb of the turret was too fresh in mind to allow any consideration of the tremors that must eventually come in descending it. That would have to wait until tomorrow, all the fear we could bear was filling us to bursting at the moment. Then, roaming inexorably from the east, loomed a huge, black rain squall. Providentially, however, right upon our route appeared a small but cozy cave, just large enough for the five of us. The "cave of the golden plover" it was called. We took a swig of water and opened a tin of sardines, and our shattered world came slowly right again, as the celestial torrents swept overhead.

This old (and slightly damaged) photograph from the Bishop Museum files shows slopes and ridges typical of the foothills of the Temehani.

After the rain the footing was more slithery than ever. This was not so bad for climbing, but it was not ten minutes before we came to a steep, downward slope which dove into a broad, flat, seemingly endless valley. The only way to maneuver was to sit down and skid over the mud, catching at grass clumps and bushes to brake the downhill race. This of course left large, wet mud-plasters on our after parts, to comfort our journey.

As we trudged across the valley, which might better be called a sunken plateau, the sun seemed suddenly to take it into his mind to speed his descent and plunge down behind the cliffs that surrounded us. We tramped on stubbornly, but at length there rose a huge rock face before us and beyond it ridges and more ridges between us and the faraway shoulder of the mountain where our precious flower lay. We came upon a strong, gushing stream running from a waterfall into a swirling pool. We were tired and hungry, and moonlight from the east was beginning to contend with sunset in the west. So we made camp, and returned the next day disappointed, without even a glimpse of the tiare apetahi.

The golden plover is one of the longest-flying migratory birds of the Pacific. He summers in Alaska and Kamchatka and winters not only in Raiatea and her neighbors but in other islands many hundreds of miles farther south.

Two years later, we started out earlier in the day, Turo and Farika, Camille and myself. The climb was no less onerous, but we were far better prepared and our new guide, a schoolboy, whose name, he said, was Bleu-Bleu, led us as before to that formidable turret. This time though, we had brought a rope which Bleu-Bleu secured at the top and which gave us some comfort as we swung ourselves upwards. (Some comfort, but not a great deal, because we found ourselves just about as vertiginous as before when we crawled again into the cave of the golden plover.) We negotiated the same broad valley, this time well ahead of the descending sun. It was curious to find the entire route so very familiar, despite the fact that two full years had passed and we had been over it only once before. There was no trace of a path or trail anywhere along the way. Evidently the mountain is very seldom climbed. We kept constantly to the ridges, even though sometimes a more circuitous passage looked less gruelling.

After that high valley with its waterfall and rambling pools had fallen far below us, we kept on mounting and descending, up and down, until at last we came to a small pocket where two or three of the coveted bushes grew and we could pick the tiare apetahi. But we soon learned that this was only a teasing foretaste, that our goal lay up and over again. Another mile it seemed, but after a steep descent on a muddy hillside, we clambered across a deep mountain torrent and there we were in Elysium!

The flowers were everywhere. Waist deep we stood amongst them, giddy now, overwhelmed by the rich masses. The buds are very large and their pale, whitish-green globules are almost as beautiful as the open flowers intermixed with them. The leaf is a heavy, luscious green with a delicately serrated edge. It is long and slender, as wide as two fingers and nearly as long as your hand. The whole bush is round and well formed, a huge pincushion, mushroomy shape. The flowers have a faint, spicey-sweet odor, but their chief beauty lies in the creamy texture of their pure white petals. The tiare apetahi dominated the whole area; there must have been acres of them. An occasional pandanus lifted its spikey tufts above them, but otherwise there seemed to be no vegetation except low-growing grasses, ferns, and small flowering plants. The bushes all seemed to grow about the same size, about three or four feet high and the same in diameter. The stems or trunks had rough bark and at their largest girth were often as thick as your wrist. They looked to be old and seemed always to be bursting with health.

We wandered amongst them in a trance until the sun began to set and it was time to make some sort of shelter for the night. Turo selected two large pandanus trees quite close to each other and joined them together with branches cut from others. (Pandanus was the only tree on these slopes and even they were so short that they hardly qualified as treelike. But they were very thick and bushy, so that their long heavy leaves, piled up and up, made a very engaging bower to look at—to look at, but as we found out most emphatically later in the night, not very engaging as a shelter.) We ate a frugal meal from tins brought with us. It was typical, indeed almost invariable, present-day Polynesian fare: bully beef, baked beans, sardines. (Every Chinese store in the islands—and every store is Chinese, because Polynesians cannot refuse to give their goods away—is stocked with these same staples, and usually with very little else.) But we were tired and hungry and eager to sleep.

Turo had brought a sheet of plastic on which, at our setting out, I had cast scornful aspersions, but when, that night, the rain squalls began we were glad to drape it over our crouched bodies, huddled together beneath the pandanus panoply. We could not lie down, because we were on a long mountain slope and the run-off of the rains kept

Everyone pronounces the pandanus a strange-looking tree. The British have named it the "screw pine" though I can see nothing screwy or piney about it. Perched as it is on a cone-shaped basket of roots (or are they downward stems to support the trunk?), it is the one "tree" that the botanists feel fairly sure was truly indigenous to the islands—that is, the Polynesians found it in residence when they first arrived. In Raiatea this was probably at least 2000 years ago, perhaps 2500.

The coconut may also have been present, but, though its seed is a champion "floater," there are many scientists who doubt it could have made its way without the aid of man all the thousands of miles from its Southeast Asian homesite, especially against the prevailing oceanic waves and currents.

The pandanus produces an edible though not very palatable fruit which was eaten in times of famine or shortage. But its long, spiky leaves make the finest mats and the best roofing thatch, so the sturdy *fara* was always much respected and still is and, I suspect, ever will be.

a constant sheet of water trickling beneath us. The only thing to do was to squat, so that as little of your body as possible was constantly wet, put your bowed head upon your folded arms, and sleep as best you could. Which was not very good. Only between squalls could we catch a quick wink. But the squalls kept coming intermittently, with hardly a pause. It was cold too, high up on the mountain, riding the trade winds.

That night was an ordeal, but somehow we survived it, waiting eagerly for the eastern light and the popping of the apetahi buds when the sun's first rays would light upon them. We heard a few faint pops, but only a few, because the squalls kept right on coming with the sun seemingly always behind them. Because the flowers stay open and unfaded for several days, there were still masses of them in spite of the scarcity of new arrivals that rainy morning.

A breakfast of gallons of steaming-hot tea and a bushel of biscuits got our soggy systems going again. Turo, Farika, and Bleu-Bleu clambered up the slopes, picking the flowers with great abandon. We cautioned restraint, but there were so many of them and new ones popping open about as fast as they could pop mature ones into their coconut-frond baskets that our conservation-conscious, New England qualms seemed out of place in that tropical prodigality. I noticed, however, that Turo paused every so often, to break off a short branch and thrust it into the soil, whenever he found an open spot. He said they would soon propagate and make up for the flowers we picked. Besides, the picking of a flower could not harm the bush.

And so we slid back down the mountain with four bursting panniers of the flowers. Toto Eb had promised to come part way up to meet us in the morning. It was he who owned the valley through which we had approached the mountain the day before. He had secured Bleu-Bleu for us, had loaned us the rope to steady our pallid spirits up the tower, and he had given us a lift on his jeep to the end of the road which ran to the top of his banana plantation, where the foothills of the Temehani begin. But there was no Toto Eb nor jeep at our trysting place, so we just

The island boat's next-to-last stop was at our little dock. From there it chugged "around the corner" of the point to tie up for the night at a small wharf built of coral heads that juts out near one of our local maraes.

kept on down, weary but hot now in the late-morning sun and before long, as is the way in these islands (and the reason why you see no raincoats and seldom an umbrella), weary, yes, but *dry*.

As we approached Toto Eb's house we saw the jeep mired to its hub caps. It had set forth but had progressed only a dozen yards. It was some comfort to us to learn that we had not been selected up there in the clouds for special punishment from the heavens, that the night's storms were the worst of the year, and that there was trouble everywhere below.

We found to our great good fortune that the island boat had not yet left, and we tumbled aboard, ready to stretch out on deck and sleep and sleep. But, no, everyone had to have a few flowers and to talk about them and sing about them and give us a swig and yet another swig of beer. No, there was no sleep until we reached home, and then there were two or three days of it, interrupted only by visits from neighbors or relatives to show us their "couronnes" (apetahi wreaths on their heads) for, surprisingly to us, almost no one in our south village had ever seen this flower from the north.

Turo's grandmother, our good neighbor who granted permission to build our remblai from her land into the lagoon. She is wearing a "couronne" of the tiare apetahi that we had just brought back from the Temehani.

Ile Tautau
ÎLE TAHAA
Mt. Puraniti
Mt. Ohiri
Mt. Tete
Mt. Maunl Roa
Be. Patio
Be. Faaaha
Be. Vaiore
Be. Tapuamu
Be. Hurepiti
Be. Haamene
Be. Apu
Be. Patii
Be. de Teonera
Haa-oa
Mt. Fareura
Vge. de Tahaa
Pte. Mamora
Pte. Tiva
Pte. Pari
Pte. Tiamahana
Pte. Apu-Pulu
Pte. Toamaro
Pte. Tepane
Pte. Patata
Pte. Rei
Pte. Mataira
Pte. Mebo
I. Mahea
I. Toahotu
Passe Toahotu
Passe Paipai
I. Fatufatu
I. Toatoatu
Gd. Be. Central
Pte. Motu Tabu
Uturoa
Mt. Tapioi
Apooiti
Upapa
Fafao
I. Tetaro
Port d'Uturoa
North Pass Lights in line 269°
Pte. Tenape
I. Tahu Naoe
Passe de Rautoanui
I. Torea
Pte. Tereia
Plateau de Temehani
Mt. Orotaio
Be. Vairahi
Be. Manuihi
Be. Averaiti
Be. Averarahi
Pte. Tainuu
Pte. Opeha
I. Hinahuruvi
I. Iriru
Passe Iriru
ÎLE RAÏATEA
Baie Faaroa
I. Horea
Passe Tiano (difficult)
I. Tiano
Be. Tetoroa
Re. Apoomau
Farepaiti
Manfenua
Fareparahi
Pte. Faainu
I. Teautavaha
Passe Teavamoa
Pte. Faatiaapiti
Toahiva
I. Outara
Be. Tehurui
Be. Vaiaeho
I. Toamaro
Passe Toamaro
Mt. Faneuhi
Vallée de Faaroa
Vallée de Toahiva
Hotopuu
South Summit
Re. Maoroa
Be. Vaiaau
Motu Tapute
Motu Paria
Motu Roa
Be. Hoapea
Be. Faarahi
Pte. Haapapa
Be. Vaihuti
Be. Tuatau
Be. Faatemu
Be. Vaianae
Passe Punaeroa
I. Haaio
Be. Tuuroto
Pte. Putete
I. Nao-Nao
Passe Nao-Nao (not very good)
Reef interspersed with coral patches, always covered
depths varying from nearly awash to 10 feet

CHAPTER THREE

Creation According to the Gospel of Modern Science

The island of Raiatea when you see it on a map is shaped like a drop of water or a tear, albeit a tear with ragged edges, narrow at the top, wide at the bottom. Above it to the north lies the round, even more ragged, island of Tahaa, and the two of them appear to be a jewelled pendant in the sea. The twin islands are surrounded by one continuous coral reef that is pierced intermittently by passes to the open sea, passes that have been caused by the funnelling of fresh waters that run down from the mountains and prevent the coral from growing as they force their way out into the salty ocean. These waters come, of course, from the never-ending procession of Trade Wind clouds which are intercepted by the mountaintops and converted into long silvery cascades that stream down the precipices and converge into tumbling, then ambling, rivers that make their inevitable way to the lagoon. This lagoon is unique as coral fringed islands go, in being navigable all the way around, inside the reef, even for a vessel drawing as much as twelve feet of water. One can easily sail through the pass between the twin islands, in from Huahine or Tahiti to the east and out to Bora Bora or Maupiti in the west. A most reassuring barrier it is, and most conveniently provided with well-spaced passes in and out to sea.

The raggedness of the shorelines of these islands is caused by deep bays or fjords which are in turn the result of the jumbled hills, ridges, mountains, valleys, craters, and crevices left by ancient volcanic action. There must at one time have been awesome convulsions, rock flying every which way, and settling into the most bizarre con-

Opposite
The islands of Raiatea and Tahaa with their common encircling reef, reproduced from a contemporary U.S. Hydrographic Office chart, which is in turn a reproduction of a French Admiralty chart.

The pinnacle at Haapapara which was seen in the distance from the window in our house on pages 18 and 19 is a striking example of naked rock, impervious to vegetation. It has about the same dimensions as the Empire State Building in New York, being roughly 1000 feet high. *Haapapara* means "ascent."

tortions. And yet over the aeons this riven rock has been coated with a lush mantle of thick green. Trees grow out from overhanging cliffs. Ferns creep to the last rays of light in deep grottoes. Thick grasses mat the sharp, steep ridges. A huge, up-thrusting spike of naked rock will occasionally defy the verdure, but for the most part soil is everywhere and life is everywhere upon it. So thick is the tangle of roots that almost no flattening erosion takes place, leaving weird fingers, knobs, and chimneypots of rock sticking up from and out of the ridges. And encircling all this rich land mass is the ever-building, live coral, making a breakwater against the pounding seas and leaving between the open sea and the land a fishpond teaming with edible life. The whole, indeed, seems divinely devised to create an ideal environment for man.

This is only a brief introductory sketch to the geography of this island, because later on I will quote at considerable length more intimate and vivid close-at-hand impressions of a much earlier visitor than myself who came to Raiatea on a whaling ship in the early 1800's. Meanwhile let us next consider the way in which this perfect setting for man was bestowed upon him.

The floor or bottom or earth surface of the Pacific Ocean is an interesting area about which little has been known until very recently; that is, until the last couple of decades. It is a huge expanse, much larger than all the continental or dry lands put together. Like dry land it has mountain ranges, valleys, ridges, plains, but unlike our often jagged landscape, its features are blurred and softened by layers of sediment built up over millions of years. Throughout the greater part of time, the great ocean's floor has been heaving, subsiding, and shifting about ever since Cretaceous times at least, some 130 million years ago. This uneven "breathing" of the ocean's vast bosom may have been going on even longer than that, but the only way, so far, we can measure these movements is by sampling the thicknesses and character of the sediments on the sea floor. These samples, taken in the form of cores by drilling or "punching" are in most cases practicable only to a depth of several meters and valid for dating no further back than the Cretaceous. Recent drillings go deeper and deeper, but their significances are only beginning to be analyzed. In any case for our present purpose, of exploring the origins and raisons d'etre of the apetahi, the Cretaceous is sufficient, since that is the era during which our present-day flowering plants were born.

The extensive ocean floor is divided into three main parts: 1) the broad, deep basin of the northern and western Pacific, which the biogeographers call "normal" or stable; 2) the so-called East Pacific Rise, which is relatively shallow and "abnormal" or unstable; and 3) the areas in between, which in some parts tend to be normal and in others abnormal. It is with this intermittent area that we are principally concerned, because here in the very middle of the ocean lie Raiatea, the Marquesas, and Rapa, the homelands of the three species of the genus *Apetahia.* And perhaps the most likely explanation of the

Table of Eras

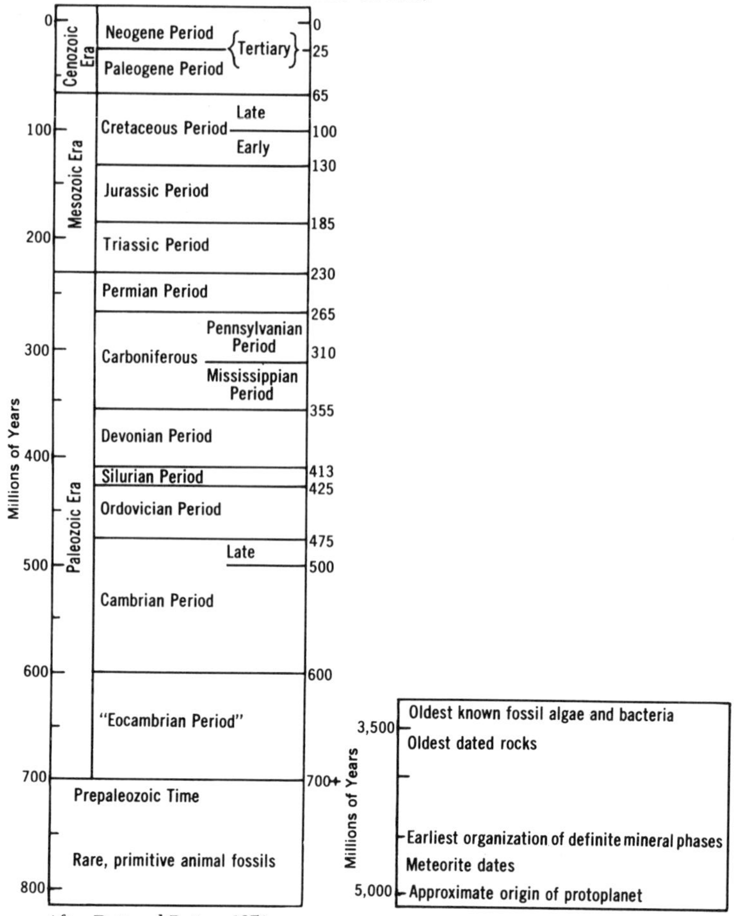

After Dott and Batten, 1971

strange distribution of our Raiatean flower and of its two widely scattered relatives is the movement, over the aeons, of the ocean floor beneath. It is a complicated explanation and even though it will be greatly simplified in this book, it will still be intricate, involving a good many seemingly diverse elements which combine or diverge to create the great cosmic geological dance that causes the many complex and, at first glance, mysterious distributions on distant oceanic islands of plants, insects, birds, lizards, and fish, but not that johnny-come-latelyest, man, and the few animals he brought with him.

Opposite
These conjectural maps of Pangaea and its evolutions were drawn by Robert MacLean from various sources, such as the *New York Times*, the *National Geographic*, the *Scientific American*, and the *Smithsonian*.

Until just a few years ago, the old theory of Gondwanaland was almost unanimously considered by scientists only an amusing myth. Gondwanaland, as the "myth" went, was the original, single land mass which later broke apart to

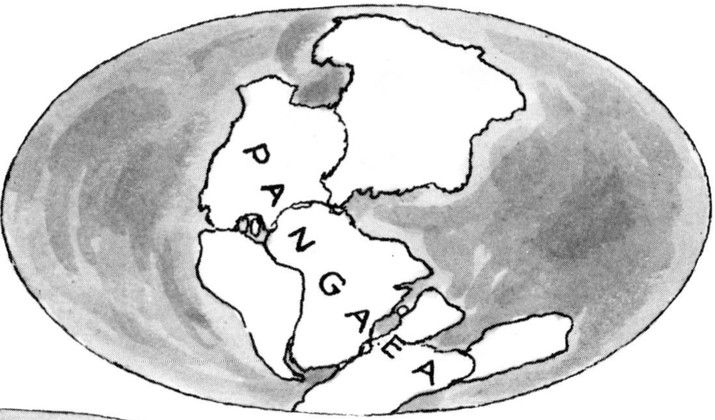

ORDOVICIAN
450 million years ago

PERMIAN
250 million years ago

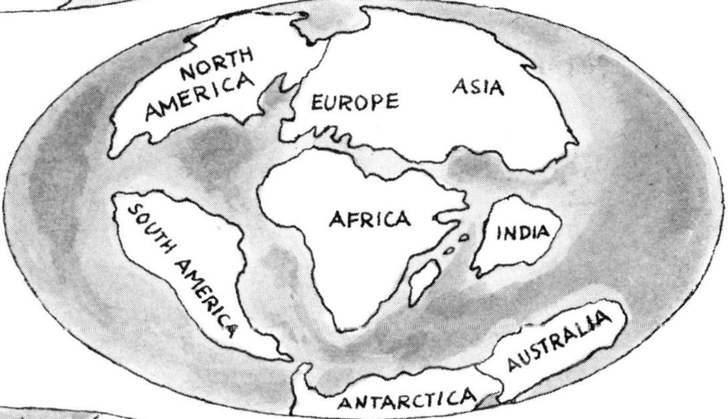

PALEOGENE
50 million years ago

NEOGENE
1 million years ago to present

form our present continental masses. When one considers the Himalayas and the Andes and the seas between them, this does seem as far-fetched as a fairy tale. But now new developments in tectonics have persuaded the earth scientists to push the continents about like pieces of a giant jigsaw puzzle. Evidently there are great and also smaller plates of relatively cool, hard, rock floating on the mobile molten rock material of the inner earth, which can carry a whole continent about like a passenger on a raft, so that not only have the lands drifted away from an original central mass, but they have drifted back again, opening and closing the oceans probably at least twice over the aeons. Of course, sections of the ocean floor are drifting about also, and rising and falling. Some of these have been carrying islands and island chains.

Now, all this is interesting geologically, to be sure, but you may well ask what it has to do with the flower of the Temehani. It is introduced here because a present-day botanist will tell you that it may be one of the most important explanations of plant dispersal, an answer, though perhaps only one of many, to why the apetahi grows only on the high slopes of the Temehani and why its only two close relatives grow only on far distant islands. *Apetahia longistigmata* is found in the crest of the cloud zone, some 3000 feet high, in the Marquesas Islands, which lie 500 miles to the northeast of Raiatea. *Apetahia margaretae* occurs on Rapa some 500 miles to the southeast with a thousand miles between. Although these three sisters are the only species in their genus *Apetahia*, which is a member of the Campanulaceae family, there is very little family resemblance. *A. raiateensis* is a handsome shrub, roughly puffball-shaped, about three or four feet high. *A. longistigmata* is a low, grassy scrub a foot or two high. *A. margaretae* is a tree, growing as tall as 30 feet. Small wonder that only a botanist could tell that they are related. I have examined dried herbarium specimens of all three species of *Apetahia* at the New York Botanical Gardens and at the Bishop Museum in Honolulu. The leaves are vaguely similar in structure, otherwise they seem to have little in common. The flower of *longistigmata* was so

Opposite
In 1935 the wide-ranging botanist Forest B. H. Brown published Volume III of his work the FLORA OF SOUTHEASTERN POLYNESIA, based on collections made by expeditions under the auspices of the Bishop Museum. This third volume contained the Dicotyledons and amongst them were recorded, for the first time, the two "sisters" of the tiare apetahi.

As you see in his caption, they were not classified by him as *Apetahia*, but as *Scelerotheca*. His drawings are the best graphic representations I have been able to find. There seem to be no photographs. The native name for *margaretae* in Rapa was *kekealuke*. He evidently found no Marquesan name for *longistigmata* where, he said, "it is rare and found only at high altitudes: not collected outside the Marquesas." *Scelerotheca* is also a Campanulaceae.

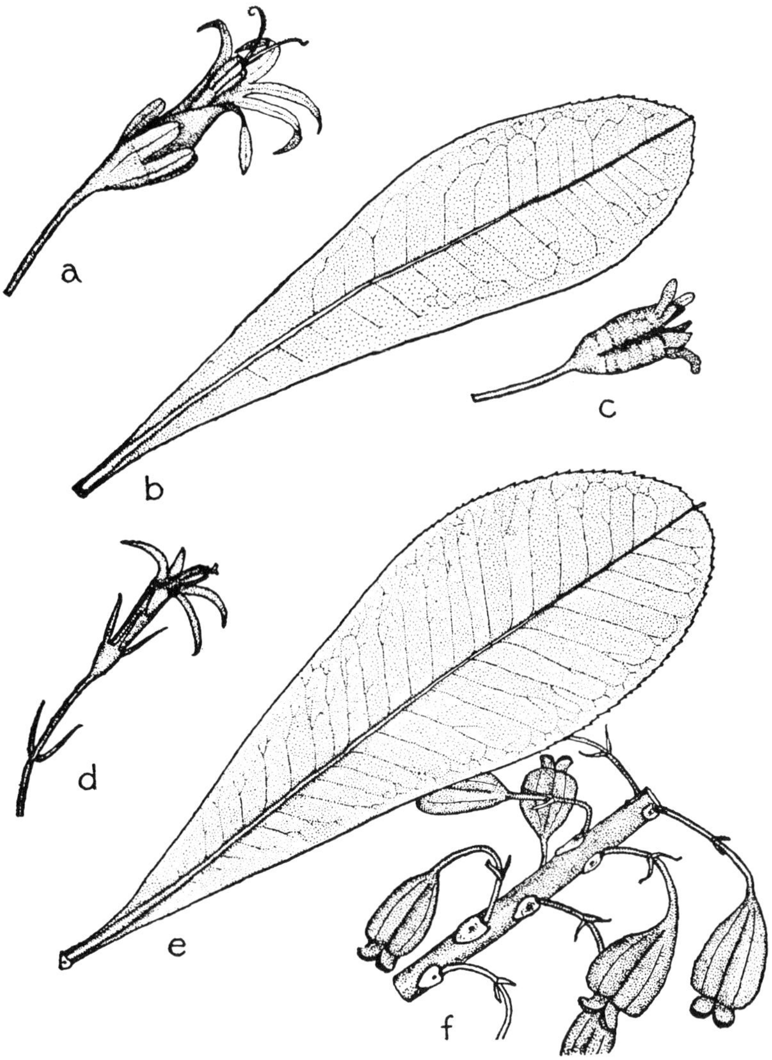

FIGURE 57.—*Sclerotheca: a-c, Sclerotheca longistigmata* F. Brown with flower (*a*), leaf (*b*), and dehisced capsule (*c*); *d-f, Sclerotheca Margaretae* F. Brown with flower (*d*), leaf (*e*), and dehisced capsules (*f*).

dried and crumpled that I could not tell if there was a "split" or not. The specimens of *margaretae* had no flowers in their folders. So here they are, these three sirens, in the very middle of the huge South Pacific Ocean with nary a clue to where they came from or how they came to be related.

Kingdom	Plantae
Phylum	Tracheophyta
Class	Angiospermae
Subclass	Dicotyledoneae
Order	Campanulales
Family	Campanulaceae
Genus	*Apetahia*
Species	*raiateensis* *longistigmata* *margaretae*

How does the botanist know of these interrelationships? Mostly by the characteristics of the flowers, but also by similarities in the leaves and stems. Here we approach the threshold of botanical classification which, however fascinating, is much too technical a subject for this book. We will simply take it on faith that these three plants are unique relatives. And that, I was surprized to discover, is often what the botanists do also. Dr. Harold St. John, who until his recent retirement, was the senior Professor of Botany at the Bishop Museum in Hawaii, told me that if he had done the classifying of this plant, he would have assigned it to the Lobeliaceae. But he also said it didn't make much difference, he knew where to locate the descriptions of its botanical details, and that was the important thing. Carlquist calls *Apetahia* a Lobeliad and relates it to *Scelerotheca* on Tahiti and Rarotonga and calls them all "lobeliads like Clermontia in their form." Forest Brown who was the first to publish *A. longistigmata* and *A. Margaretae* in 1935, originally classified them as *Scelerotheca.* They were later shifted to the genus *Apetahia.* Carlquist transfers *marga* back to *Scelerotheca*, but leaves *longi* with *Apetahia.* Very recently (1975) I was informed that the botanists at Harvard want to return both of them to their originally published lineage. It is all very confusing to the amateur and our Raiateen beauty may wind up with the very rare distinction of being a genus (or should we say gena?) all of her own. But for the time being I shall write of the three as I saw them in their herbarium folders.

Let us at least accept *A. raiateensis* as a member of the Campanulaeceae family, even though, when you compare it to a bluebell you cannot see the slightest resemblance. (Since Linnaeus listed 50 species of Campanulas in 1764, de Candolle listed 330 in 1830, and according to Hylander, 1000 species are recognized today, it has plenty of company, although as flower families go, this is one of the smaller, more exclusive ones.) But had the three sisters, if so they are, a common ancestor? How did they arrive at their dwelling places, so far apart with so much ocean waste between? Why did they scorn other islands between their distant outposts? These and many more are intriguing questions about plant dispersal, plant genetics, and plant evolution, all of them very complex subjects, but clothed in enough mystery and involving enough disagreement among scientists so that we might do a little speculating or at least review some of the speculations which have been advanced.

When I questioned some botanist friends of mine, they immediately said that continental drift was the most likely explanation, that the ancestress of most endemics sent her offspring adrift in different directions on different continents. These, over the ages, adapted themselves differently to different soils and different climates and thus *Apetahia* evolved into the three different but related species of its genus or clan.

An endemic is a plant that occurs only in one or several distinctive areas and is generally unrelated or only very distantly related to other plants surrounding it. Plants of the continental masses tend to interbreed and lose their individuality. Many endemics are rather fragile, specialized creations thus vulnerable to competition, and sooner or later they are usually overwhelmed and extinguished. Sherwin Carlquist, who is one of our best-informed and imaginative authorities on the subject, calls them "delicate products of evolutionary campaigns won without opposition." Endemics inhabit isolated areas; they are the "loners" of the plants of the earth. Mountaintops or slopes, cut-off valleys, odd spots of unusual soils or climates present us with continental spectaculars, such as the Saguaro cactus, found only in the Sonoran area in Arizona, and the

Monterey cypress, confined to the Monterey peninsula in California. But the choicest dwelling places for endemics are, naturally enough, small islands surrounded by ample ocean water, and on these are found such freaks as the elephant tree of Socotra, the silver-swords of Halekala, Hawaii, the Traveller's "palm" of Madagascar, the Coco de Mer of the Seychelles (with its largest of all seeds, a double "coconut" that is not a coconut), and many others.

As one ranges around the earth, spotting endemics, it becomes evident that our *Apetahia* is not as extraordinary and inexplicable as it seemed when we first encountered it on the Temehani. There are not a great many true endemics, but there are enough so that, even though they differ from each other much more than the vast majority of plants, they can be set apart as a class of their own, geniuses or failures or in-betweens, but not of the common crowd.

Now continental drift seems a likely enough way to account for these botanical evolutions in isolated environments and on relatively nearby or offshore islands, even if these islands have become fenced off over the ages by cold ocean currents or hot, dry winds or special soil conditions. (Born on the mainland, they spread to the outskirts, then drifted off on their respective land rafts to evolve in isolation their own distinctive and often weird personali-

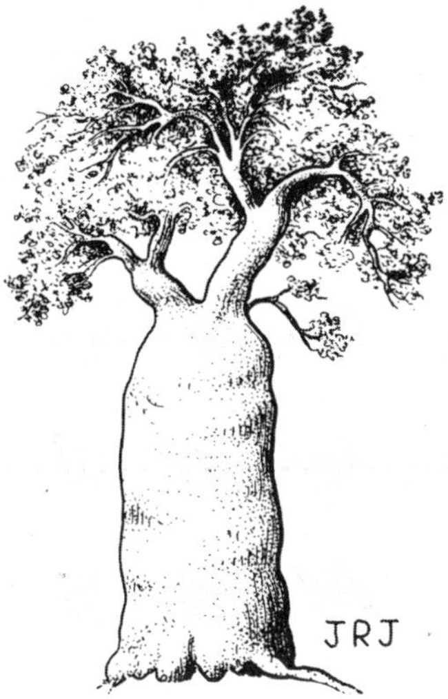

Six strange plants illustrative of of endemics: the Saguaro cactus (*far left*) and the Monterey cypress (*opposite below*) are both photographs by Edwin Way Teale. *Above*: the Traveller's palm, the Elephant tree, and the Silver-sword. *Below*: the Coco de Mer.

ties.) But how about three islands in the middle of the Pacific? When one looks at the conjectural map of Gondwanaland, or Pangaea as it is now more commonly named, it becomes apparent to anyone with a geographical turn of mind that the center of this "original" landmass is roughly Mesopotamia or Afghanistan, and that when the continents were all gathered together this, their central area, must have been on the side of the globe almost directly or equilaterally opposite to the area of our triangle of islands, Raiatea, Nuku Hiva, and Rapa. Then think of the then size of the "Pacific" ocean! It must have been all the water of the world in one, 71 percent, or nearly three times larger than the whole of Pangaea. It seems inconceivable that an ancestral plant originating on such a landmass could send its offspring over such monstrous stretches of salt sea. Surely, for the tiare apetahi, continental drift is much more unlikely an explanation than it is say for *Bubbia*, which occurs in Australia, New Guinea, and even Madagascar—and which probably once stretched from Africa across Asia into the Pacific, but has died out on the continents.

There are, however, other means available to plants for long-distance dispersal. Wind carries pollen and spores extraordinary distances. Ocean currents have born coconuts and other floaters a long way. Birds fly with seeds stuck in mud to their feet, even wedged in crevices of their feathers. They also carry them undigested in their intestines. But for the distances that concern us here these are not likely transportation agents. So, for our most tempting possibility we are left with the most controversial one: land bridges or island chains. And this brings us back to tectonics or shifting plates of the earth's crust—not the subterranean plates that carry the continents, but the submarine plates that shift the configurations of the ocean floor.

From newly discovered evidence of ancient guyots and seamounts, of plateaus and trenches, and from present-day evidence of islands above the surface, it can be assumed that these tectonic areas have always been sprinkled with volcanic cones, welling up like giant pimples from the underlying molten viscous mass. They erupt to

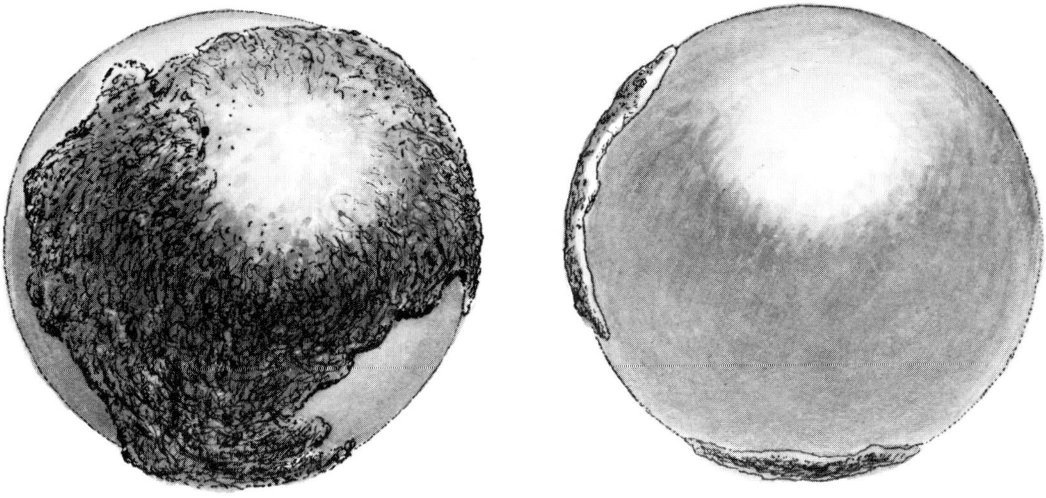

Pangaea and Panthalassa. Since the ancestress of the tiare apetahi would have had to place the genes of her descendant in the very middle of Panthalassa, continental land must have been as far away as possible in all directions. Her progeny would have had a lot of traveling to do.

build high islands. They are eroded to form seamounts. They subside to become guyots or the foundations of coral atolls. They rise again to become flat coral islands, like those of Tonga.

Until recently it was believed that volcanic cones spouting upward from the bottom eventually sank back under their own weight to form barrier reefs and coral atolls. This was Darwin's explanation, at a time when plates and tectonics were unknown, and he was, of course, the first, or at least the most eminent, early student of this variegated phenomenon. Now it is commonly believed that a volcano wells up through a submarine rock plate and then is carried by it very gradually into deeper water, thus forming reefs or atolls, and later moves back into shallow water, to create up-risen coral islands. No volcano, it is argued, is massive enough to sink through a plate or to bear the plate itself downward by its gravitational weight. This seems likely enough once you accept the theory that these plates carry whole continents merrily about.

All of this heaving, subsiding, clashing, and drifting takes place so slowly, over such far reaches of time, that plants have time to populate them all—not all plants, not even many reach the farthest distant salients, for frequencies of species decrease noticeably as they extend their ranges beyond their continental origins, but a large enough number travel the ultimate reach so that their presence in the end is a wonder that sets the botanist to marvelling—and also to quarrelling with his fellows about how this wonder could come to pass. And the product of such a wonder is our *Apetahia raiateensis*, a lone genus at the very end of the chain.

This "end of the chain" is not tossed in here merely as hyperbole. It is also, in a literal sense, the essence of the "quarrelling" between the scientists. There are those who argue, heatedly and learnedly, for land bridges and island chains over which such plants as the *Apetahia*'s ancestress could have disseminated gradually or hopped from crest to nearby crest. And there are those who contend just as hotly and authoritatively that such transportation facilities never existed. At present the resolution to the debate awaits more knowledge of the sea floor, and the oceanographers are busy collecting it. Their extraordinary work so

This interesting speculative map is taken from a monograph by H. W. Menard and Edwin L. Hamilton, entitled "Paleogeography of the Tropical Pacific." It is included in PACIFIC BASIN BIOGEOGRAPHY; *A Symposium*, edited by J. Linsey Gressitt and published by the Bishop Museum Press in 1963.

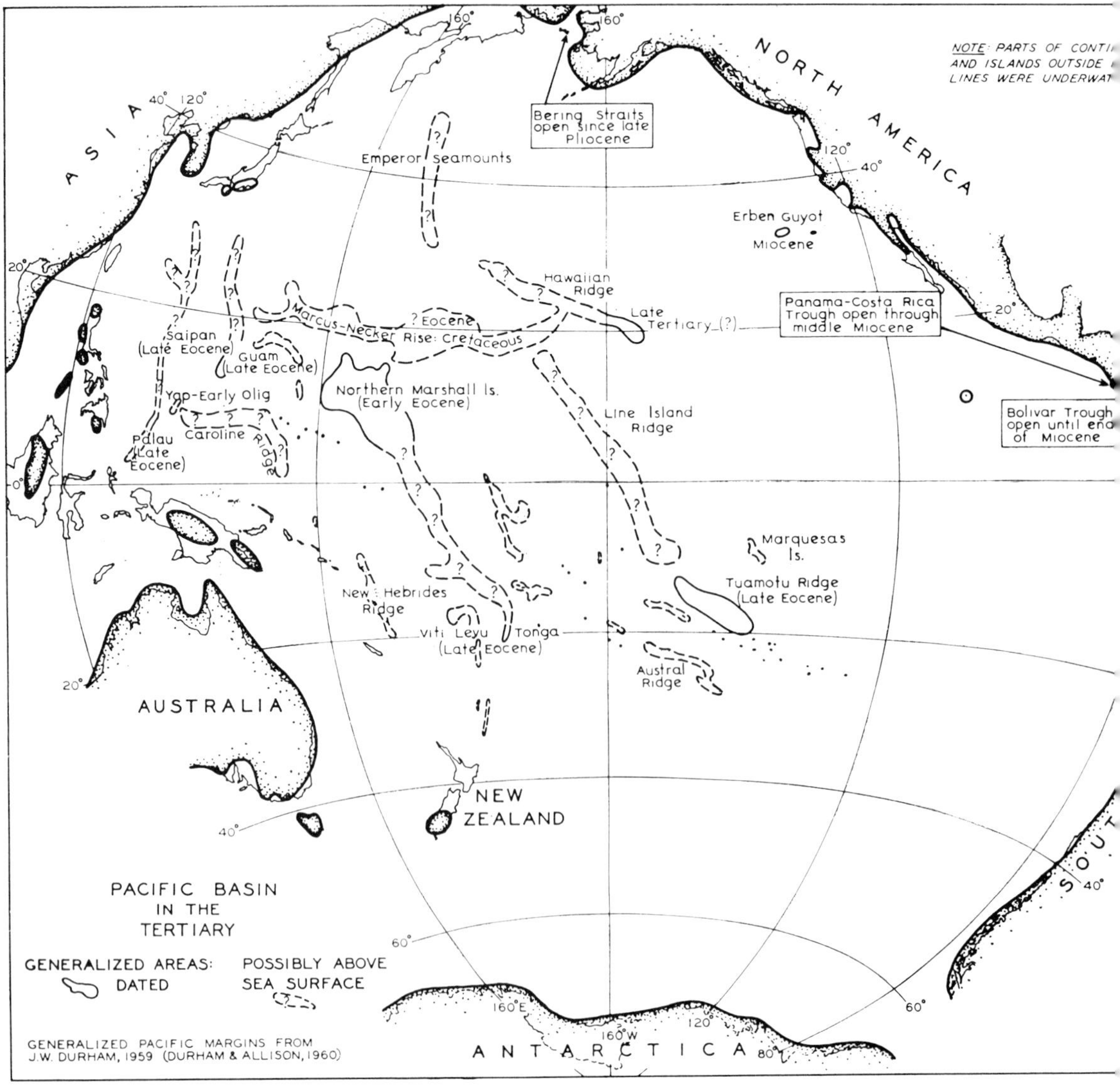

far, just since the end of the Second World War, has already opened a pandora's box. And yet they feel they have not yet even scratched that immense subsurface. It will take many more years and much more support for research, but my guess is that the "chainers," or "bridgers," or advocates of lost peninsulas will win, and that this theory is the most likely explanation of the existence of our three miraculous *Apetahia* sisters.

Another speculation that I have been flirting with is an erstwhile huge island that the Tuamotu archipelago must very probably have been some six million years ago. Those 80 odd atolls, great and small, must at one time have been lofty mountain peaks, very possibly joined together at their bases by valleys and ridges. The whole mass would have run a thousand miles in length, northwest to southeast and 3 hundred miles in breadth. Can one imagine the island of Madagascar, there in the middle of the ocean those millions and millions of years ago? It would have been lavishly populated with plants and birds and insects and surrounded with myriads of fish.

Then it starts to sink, the whole of it (or rather the tectonic plate on which its volcanoes have erected themselves). Over the aeons it subsides until only the tips of the highest mountain peaks show above the level of the sea. The coral builds rings around them as they settle. And when they have disappeared a thousand feet below the surface, the coral ring of the atoll is all that is left, all we see today (except perhaps in the single instance of Mangareva where the pinnacle of their Everest still protrudes above the ocean swells).

Someday there may be enough paleontological retrieval from that multitude of lost volcanoes to give us some inkling of the life that existed upon that great lost ocean island. Meanwhile we know only that, from samples of submarine volcanic rock taken recently by the French in their search for atom bomb test sites, the rock is probably about six million years old. The Marquesas, another lost island several hundred miles to the northeast are probably several million years old also. But we don't know how many. Tahiti to the southwest is some two million years. Raiatea, still another 100 miles westward is a bit

The Bristle-thighed Curlew or his ancestor may have been a bird who brought the first seed of the apetahi to Raiatea. Carlquist is a strong advocate of dispersion by birds. My choice of this one is romantic, not scientific. His proper name is *Numénius tahitiensis*, meaning that he was the only curlew discovered in the Tahitian islands. He is a very long-distance migrator since he breeds in Alaska, but he may have needed island chains to reach as far as Raiatea. He is a berry eater, so he could have carried a seed in his stomach, but it also seems conceivable that one might have wedged in the bristles of his thighs. We will never know.

Later, and much more scientifically significant, evidence has just come from deep-sea drillings by the *Glomar Challenger* whose cores from the ocean floor show that the Tuamotu archipelago is at least 50 million yeares old. Perhaps the French tests were taken on volcanoes of much more recent origin in that area.

older but probably only a mere million years. Rapa to the southwest is another question mark.

So the ancestress of our *Apetahia* could conceivably have evolved on the huge lost island of "Tuamotua," dispersed her offspring as she sank below the waters to her younger neighbors, north, south and west before she slipped to her watery grave. They in turn would have adapted themselves differently to their different environments. Many cousins on in-between islands would have dropped out of the race, and over the millenia our three sisters would have undergone so many sea changes that there is little likelihood they could recognize each other today. (Only a very acute and very snoopy modern botanist could do that.) And thus this little family may have come to consist, today, of the scrubby-like, littlest sister on the Marquesas, the tall, gawky one on Rapa, and our own scintillating Cinderella of Raiatea.

Their physical diversities are easier to explain and are subject to little disagreement. The interworkings of genetic evolution and isolated environments are known to produce variants differing radically from their root stocks. Basic principles are now recognized, but the hows and whys have many mysteries to be tidied up. One of these is

Robert MacLean, again from various sources, has illustrated six different stages or phases of the formation and evolution of oceanic islands and their coral, based on recent tectonic theories.

the mystery of how the tiare apetahi is fertilized and propagated. A botanist must live a long time with a flower to learn such secrets, and in this case he cannot bring it to his laboratory greenhouse. He must pitch his tent and keep himself alive for months or perhaps years, high on the shoulders of the Temehani. No one has done so, as yet.*

This, then, to recapitulate, is the geologic history of our island. First, if we can imagine a cross section of an arc of the earth in the mid-Pacific, we see a heavy, hardrock plate floating upon the fiery molten rock below it. At some point of time which our present-day techniques cannot measure, but which we know is fairly recent compared to the continental upheavals (even though it must be many millions of years ago, perhaps hundreds of millions), a weak spot in this plate allows a spout of the underlying

* The various possibilities from which this hypothetical lonely scientist on the Temehani might choose, look to the layman like a fascinating botanical smorgasbord for he may select from such offerings as heterozygosity, genetic momentum, ecological adaptations, lessened dispersibility, pricinctiveness, constancy of pollinators, autogamy, dioecious, monoecious, and gynodioecious interfertile speciation, hybrid swarms and fertile recombinants, autochthonous floral morphology, anemophilous species, and perhaps a few others.

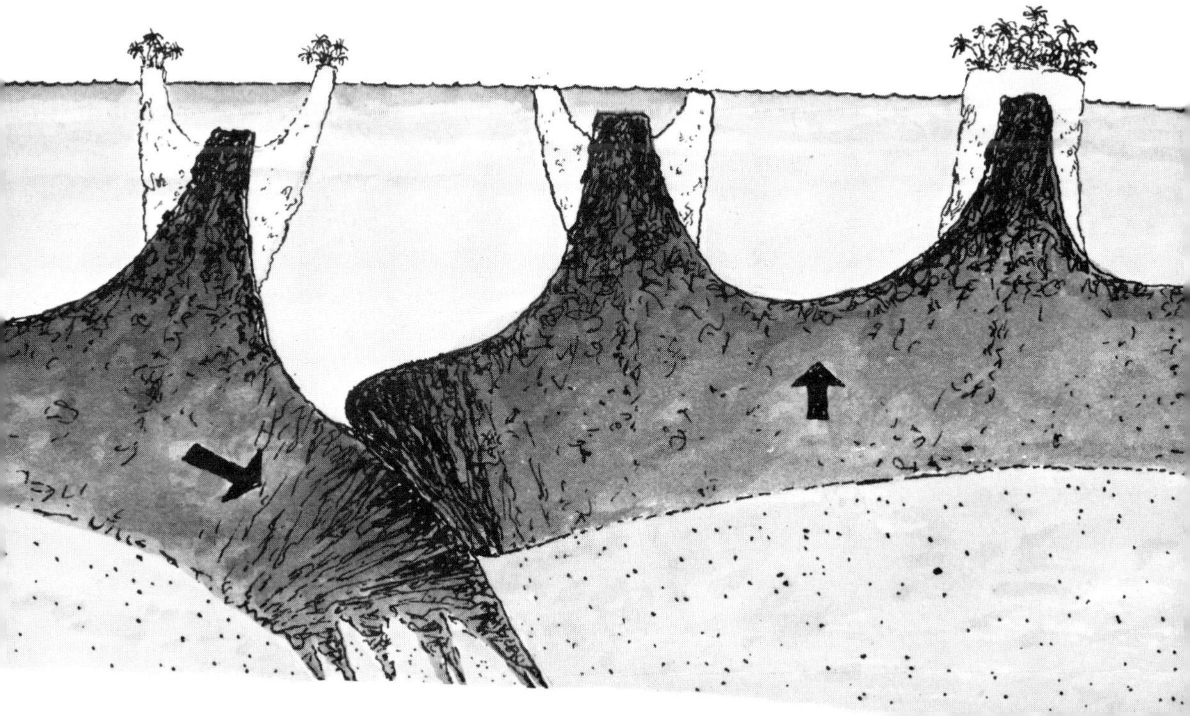

molten rock to force its way upward, through the plate and through the ocean, up into the air above, some thousands of feet up, hardening as it mounts upward and flows outward, jagged and irregular, but roughly conical in shape from its base on the plate to its summit in the sky. When this final height is reached, the inner core usually subsides, leaving a crater, either round or fragmentary and the walls or portions of walls of that crater are our island.

The plate moves on, jostling and contending with other plates, much as ice floes struggle with each other on the Arctic seas. When two are pushed irresistibly together, one must buckle under the other and thus sink slowly into the ocean floor. As it does sink, it naturally bears our island down with it. During this infinitesimally slow process, billions upon billions of minute coralline animals build upon each other, live ones always seeking the light and air and nourishing wave water of the surface of the sea. As the island slowly sinks, the live coral dies and hardens to support new life above. And in this way the reef that encircles the island is formed over the aeons.

As the plate supporting our island sinks, its contender is rising and its coralline islands rise above the sea. If they had previously sunk sufficiently so that their rock cones had disappeared completely beneath the surface, they would have become atolls, rings of coral around a central lagoon. And if these atolls had risen, the lagoons would have been filled in by wave action with the debris of the coral, dying as it rose, to become such high coral islands as Tongatabu and Guam. But contending plates, one rising up, the other thrust down, is not the only way that these various types of islands can be formed. Non-contending plates can drift or be pushed or be sucked about the ocean floor, always afloat on the mobile rock-sea beneath them, so that they move into deeper or shallower depths of the ocean's water with the same coralline processes taking place.

All of this, it must be kept in mind, is the creation of our island according to modern science. Now let us have a look at it according to the ancient Polynesian.

CHAPTER FOUR

Creation According to the Gospel of Raiatea

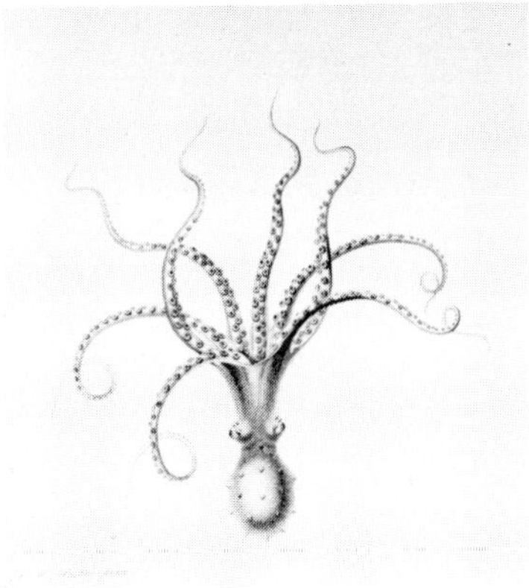

Of course the Polynesian would have had to arrive at his island before he could conceive of its creation, so before writing about his creation concept, let us skip forward to how and when he got there, and then go back to how and when the island was created for him.

Polynesian origins and the settlement of the ocean islands have given rise to much speculation and much conflicting argument ever since the European "discovered" them some 200 years ago. Only a couple of decades past there was room for lively dispute, Thor Heyerdahl claiming the Polynesians came from America, Andrew Sharp claiming the islands could have been settled only by accidental blow-aways. Now, at last, the linguists, geneticists, archaeologists, and other anthropological scientists pioneered by Kenneth Emory have at last resolved the matter and their findings have been confirmed by elaborate computer analysis only this last year. A brief summary will do.

The root stock of the Raiateans (and all other Polynesians) originated in Southeast Asia and migrated some 2500 years ago, by way of the Indonesian and Melanesian archipelagoes, to the West Polynesian island groups of Fiji, Samoa, and Tonga. From there they sailed (and paddled) in large, ocean-going double canoes on intentional voyages of discovery, first tc the central Polynesian groups of the Marquesas, Tuamotus, and Society Islands. There they probably paused a few centuries to consoli-

Current hypotheses, especially those of W. W. Howells, plead for a Micronesian avenue from Asia. A selection of Polynesian outliers is spotlighted in the west on the map on the two following pages.

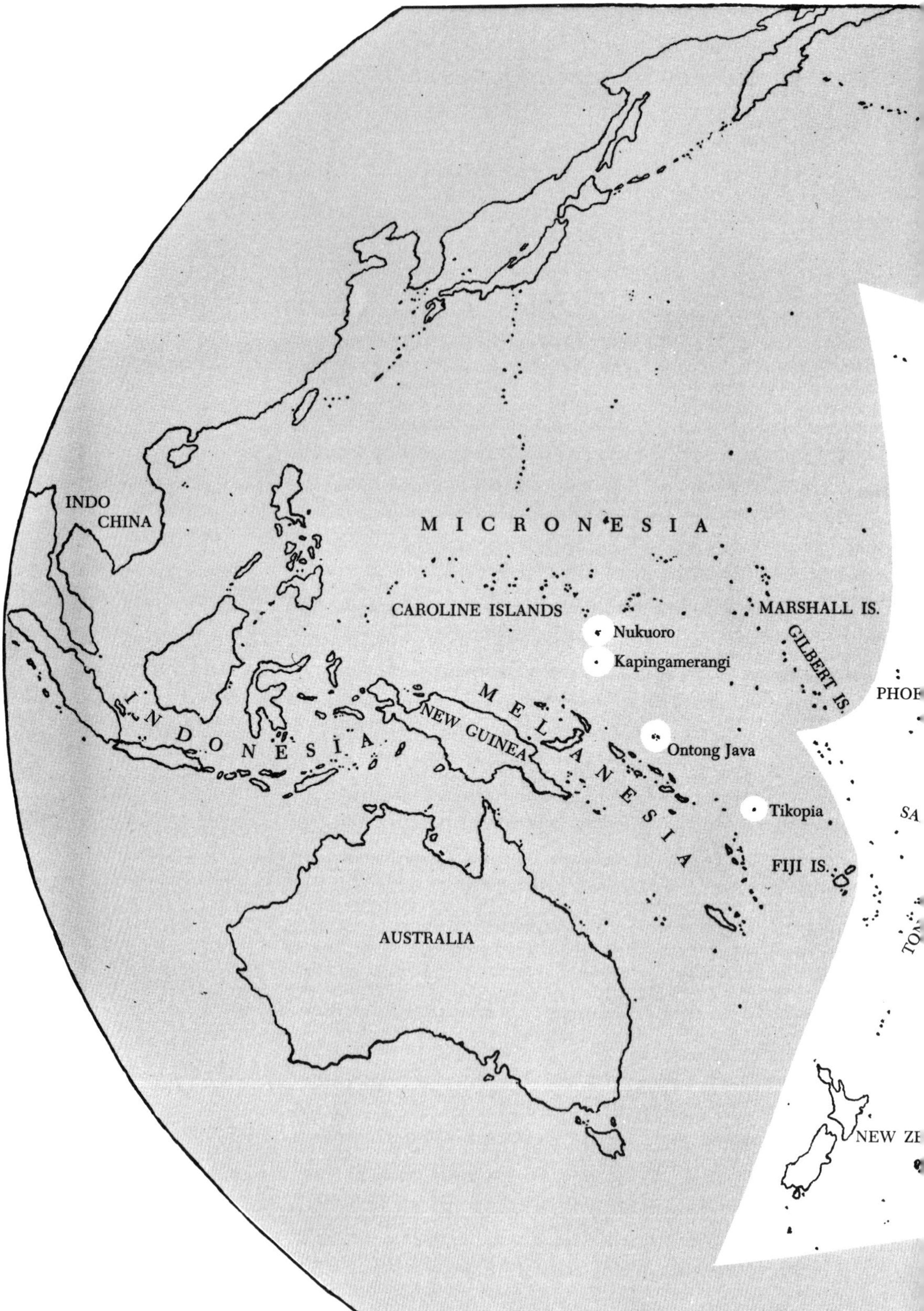

INDO
CHINA
MICRONESIA
CAROLINE ISLANDS
Nukuoro
Kapingamerangi
MARSHALL IS.
GILBERT IS.
INDONESIA
NEW GUINEA
MELANESIA
Ontong Java
Tikopia
FIJI IS.
AUSTRALIA

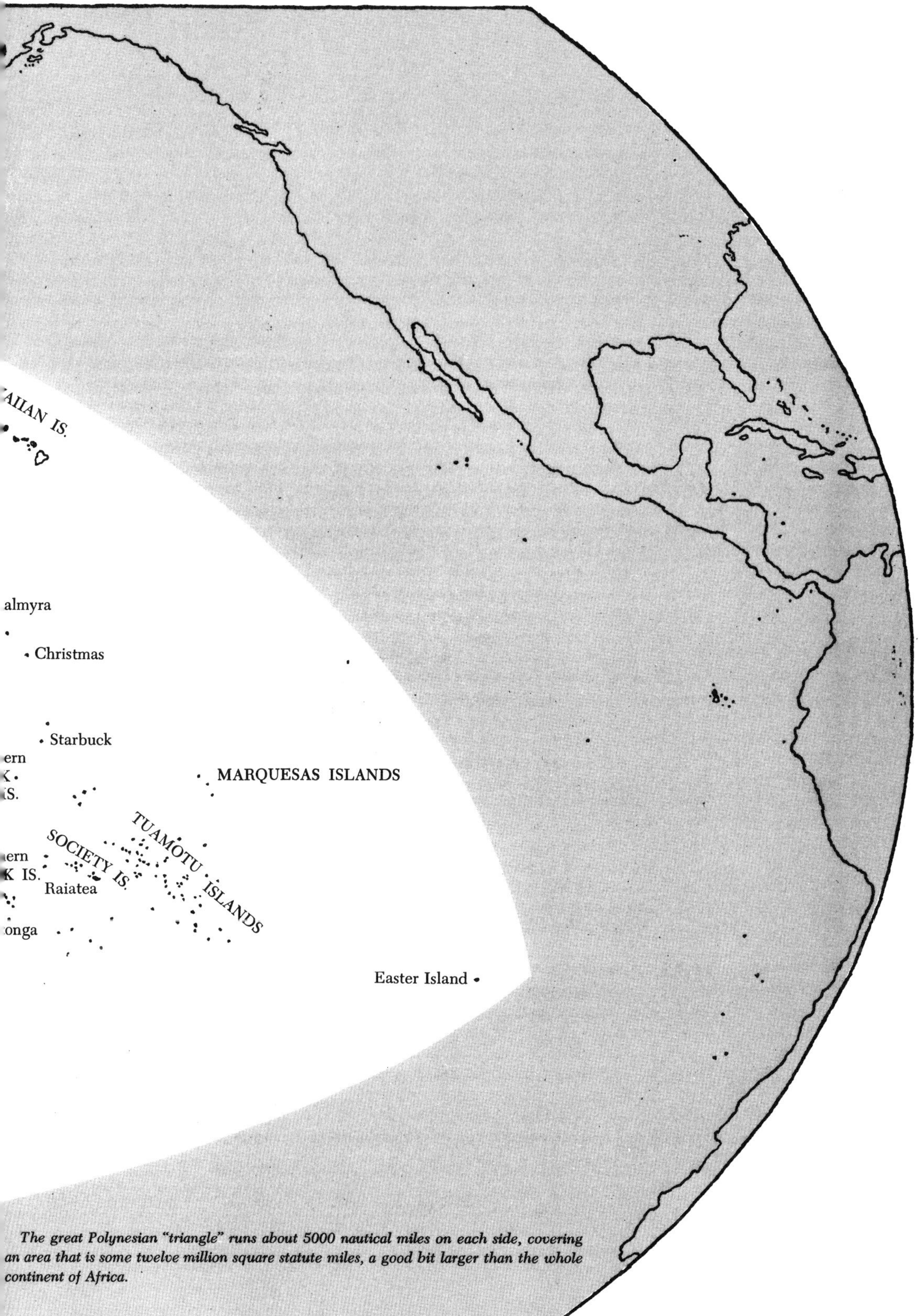

The great Polynesian "triangle" runs about 5000 nautical miles on each side, covering an area that is some twelve million square statute miles, a good bit larger than the whole continent of Africa.

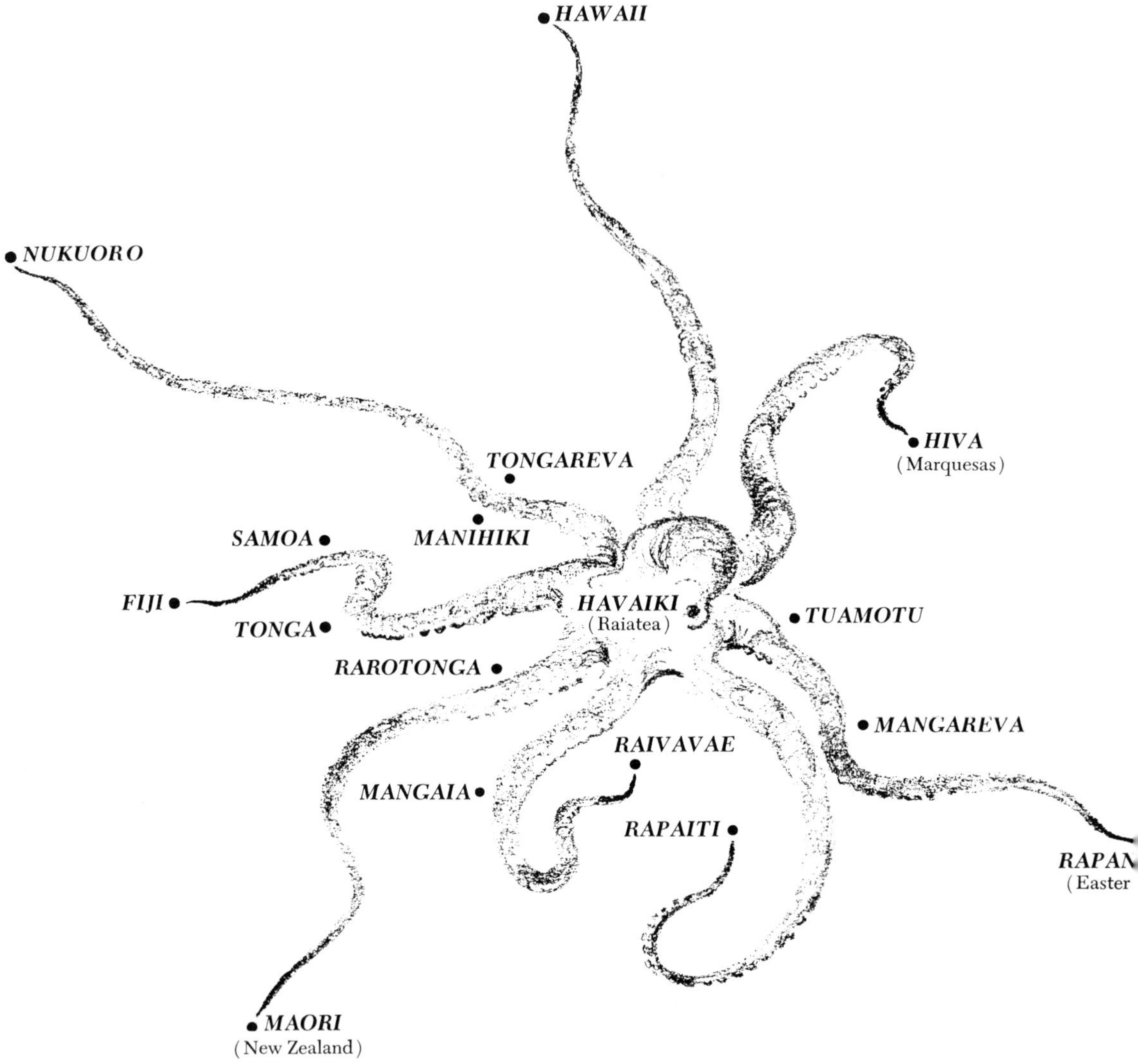

This rendition of the traditional Polynesian octopus is adapted from Te Rangi Hiroa (Sir Peter Buck).

date, refine, or perhaps even to originate the uniqueness of their culture, as the European found that culture in the 18th Century. But long before that the tentacles of the traditional Polynesian octopus had reached up north to Hawaii, southeast to Mangareva and its neighbors, east to Easter Island, south and southwest to the Australs and Cooks; then to New Zealand last of all, probably some 500 years before the European came.

The Polynesians had a custom of carrying three homeland names to three key islands in almost all of the groups that were settled by them. The names were Havaiki, Uporu, and Vavau. We find them in the "home" islands of Tonga, where Havaiki has become Ha'apai. Vavau remains as originally named. Uporu has probably been renamed. In the Samoan islands are Savaii and Upolu. Tutuila was perhaps originally Vavau. In the central islands the original Havaiki was changed to Raiatea, Uporu to Tahaa, and Vavau to Pora Pora (Bora Bora as it is commonly known today is a corruption: the old Tahitian language had no B).

It is a private hunch of mine that the first-sighted island was named Havaiki, but I have no real evidence for this supposition. It just seems a logical choice for a navigator discovering, say, either the leeward group of the Societies or the Hawaiian chain. Hawaii is the best known of the Havaikis. Upolu is a section of the big island. Vavau is lost. The presence of these names in the Hawaiian group leads one at first to speculate whether this is evidence of primary settlement from Tahiti, rather than from the Marquesas, as is nowadays the origin preferred by most anthropologists. Perhaps a more likely explanation is that secondary settlers from Tahiti, finding other islands, such as Maui and Oahu (a Marquesan-like name), already occupied, chose the big island and named it after their homeland. The Marquesas, originally the Hiva islands (Nuku Hiva, Hiva Oa, Fatuhiva), are an exception to this cardinal island-naming custom. "Hiva" means clan. Their islands may have been first settled and named by a family that migrated or were ostracized, hence they rejected the traditional old names and used their own private ones.

This is an admittedly biased argument. I am not trying to suggest an answer to the whole complex riddle of migration to the central Pacific. I want only to point out the possible significance of one island, Raiatea, a significant island, all will concede. Wherein lies that significance? Take this merely as a plea for consideration of special merits, not by any means an overall solution such as Heyerdahl advocated when he claimed that all Polynesia was settled, not from the west (as it was), but from the east. Or consider the significance of Raiatea not in the light of priority of settlement, a physical feat, but in its metaphysical predominance of all the central islands. Whenever its people came, or wherever they came from, their quality was all high, they were the princes, spiritual and temporal, of all the island groups in their constellation.

Havaiki to the Polynesians meant the homeland, the land of origin and also the land to which the spirits went after death. It has usually been translated as heaven, but I think that western concept gives it a wrong twist. To be sure, his afterworld was to the Polynesian a pleasant place, a place where food was plentiful, the air clear and refreshing, the water sweet and cool, having the attributes of all the things which appealed to Polynesian senses and besides that, significantly enough, all spirits were equal there. In real life his society was strictly hierarchized. At the top were the "arii" or high-born chiefs, who married only into their own ranks. There were certain convenient exceptions, of course, but normally if a bemused princess fell in love with a handsome commoner, it was not at all exceptional for her father, the high chief, to have the swain slaughtered as a sacrifice to the gods. The princess wept, the low-born parents mourned, but all accepted, knowing beforehand that, in spite of entreaties and advice and commands, the outcome was inevitable . . . unless the couple fled to another land or unless the lover could change himself into a shark by day and make rendezvous with his loved one in secret coves at night.

Ranking almost with the arii were the "ta'ua" (tahunga = Maori, tahuna = Tuamotu, kaula = Hawaii) usually translated as priests, but wise men or maestros might be a better definition. Sometimes the high chief was also the taua, if he was smart enough, as was often the case. And, if neither he nor his own children qualified for this high intellectual estate, he might adopt a brilliant one from the ranks as his son and thus elevate him, perhaps even to primary succession. In this way the blood lines of the "royalty" were occasionally refreshed.

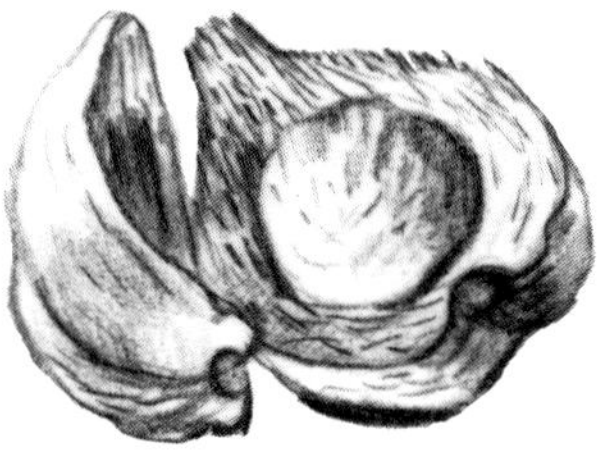

After the arii and the taua came the "ra'atira," which is sometimes translated as nobles and sometimes as gentlemen. Mainly these were the landowners or the holders of land belonging to the arii. Land to the Polynesian was the basis of all wealth, power, and prestige. It could be come by only through inheritance. Even if land were seized in combat, the conquering chief had to marry his dead opponent's wife, sister, or daughter before the conquered territory became truly his. And only his issue by such marriage could sit in the place of honor on the traditional "marae" (temple) of the land.

After these three "upper classes" came the "manahune," translated as plebians or slaves or common people. They were of the lowest order, and by far the most numerous. But even the manahune had inherent rights of no little consequence. Mostly these rights were negative ones. The local chief (raatira) depended on them of course, to work his land, provide his food, build his house and his canoe. If, however, a raatira mistreated his serfs, they could quit his service, move to the land of a neighboring chief, and leave him stranded. Rarely, if ever, would one of their confreres take the place of the disaffecting one. Accordingly, the chief had to mind his manners and to conduct his affairs in a fashion becoming to a chief.

Teuira Henry gives us an example of a still more conclusive way of keeping a chief in line:

"Te-mehani-ave-arii has several open winding craters, and in the largest of them people say once existed a ferocious monster, which no one ever saw, but of which there were frequent proofs in newly disturbed earth and ferns around the crater.

"On one occasion, it happened that a king named Taie, who was much hated by his people for his tyranny, went up with a party of his subjects determined to explore the crater and ascertain what kind of creature dwelt there. He had a long strong rope, and being the bravest man in the party, attached himself to one end of it, telling his men to hold the other end to pull him up quickly when he gave the signal by jerking a small rope attached to the upper end of the big one and hanging by his side.

"With this understanding while the men held on, the king descended and disappeared in the labyrinth below. Soon he violently jerked the signal rope, but no heed was paid; and he continued doing so for some time, till gradually the pulling ceased. After waiting still longer the treacherous attendants drew up their king, whom they found with his flesh devoured from his bones. They carried home what remained of him, saying as they did so, "*Ua ora ra te fenua i teie nei ari'i ino*" (The land is now free of this bad king), which was ever afterwards regarded as a terrible warning to other kings against despotism."

All of this complex structure of Polynesian life was, of course, believed to have been decreed by and to be presided over by the gods. The concept was that a god should, providing he was adequately revered and propitiated, serve men, rather than the reverse as we Westerners are wont. For instance, if a certain god did not bring a petitioner sufficient luck in fishing, he would abandon that god and transfer his devotions to another one. There were plenty of gods, and they needed supplicants as much as landlords needed laborers. So there was a certain balance and freedom of action for even the humblest—in the celestial, as well as the terrestrial, realms.

In essence all of this meant that the law of the society was a sense of fairness and the right of the whole society. By mutual consent law was interpreted by the chief, but if his judgments were deemed unfair he could be deposed. His basic right to judgment rested upon the consent of his constituency.

And so we come onto familiar ground and find that the Polynesian society was much the same as any other society the world around. The difference, and it is an interesting one, is that the Polynesian did not write things down and, thus, there was no such thing as the letter of the law and no such thing as a lawyer. Or perhaps it would be better to say that laws were conventions, and every man was his own lawyer and every chief his judge. At any rate, it resulted in a societal fabric that was supple and pliable, responsive to whims and impulses—and also to passions. To some, such a life would seem to be paradise, to others it would seem to be hell. To us, safely removed, its fascination is the observation of man living in a uniquely benevolent land, more closely attuned to primeval nature than any other of his fellow homo sapiens the world around.

Whether the first pioneers from the western Fiji-Samoa-Tonga complex went to the Marquesas or to the Societies, we shall probably never know. Regardless of priority, I believe these later two groups were settled by separate expeditions and not, as some contend, by emigration initially to the Marquesas and subsequently back southwestward, through the Tuamotus to Tahiti and the rest of the Societies. One of the main reasons for my conviction is that ancient name of Raiatea, Havaiki. Any voyage sailing east from those distant original three groups in the western Pacific would make its first landfall in the Marquesas if it bore roughly 10° north of east; in the Societies if it bore due east. The less northerly voyage, hitting the Societies, would raise Raiatea first of all* and following an-

* Maupiti, some 40 miles west of Raiatea, would have been sighted first, but when approached closely the inhospitability of its maze of coral reefs to canoes wishing to land would be readily evident, and by then the considerably larger mass of Raiatea would have loomed its welcome in the distance.

I like to think that this fifty-year-old photograph from the Bishop Museum files shows us Raiatea as she would have loomed in the distance to the Polynesians when their canoes first approached her shores, perhaps at about the same time that the warships of Xerxes were approaching the island of Salamis in the Aegean.

cient custom would have named it Havaiki after the homeland. By contrast, a voyage southwest from the Marquesas, through the Tuamotus, would have picked up Tahiti first. The Marquesans might not have named Tahiti Havaiki because they gave this traditional name to none of their own islands. As previously noted their own islands were named for their clan, Hiva, and most likely they would have made Tahiti a Hiva member too. But, then, how did Raiatea get its name, except by separate discovery? Not only Raiatea (Havaiki), but Tahaa (Uporu) and Bora Bora (Vavau)? The original names of all these islands are those in parentheses. The present names have evolved through numerous changes.

This naming seems to me one good argument for separate discovery. Another is the fact that Raiatea was the "holy land" of all central Polynesia, including the Marquesas, and Raiatea's chiefs of the red girdle held the

highest secular rank of the whole complex. Why such special honors for a relatively small island that would have been among the last discovered if the discoverers had come from the Marquesas?

So now, to my satisfaction at least, we have got Raiatea settled independently, although not necessarily firstly, and named traditionally by a voyage of explorers from Tonga, Samoa, or Fiji. (By the looks of our central Polynesian islanders' faces and their physiques they seem most likely to have come from Samoa.)

One of the first things those earliest Raiateans would ask their high priests, or taua, would be: what are the origins of this old land which we have just discovered? It might have taken the taua several generations to work out an answer to such mysteries, but here it is, refined over many, many generations, as our missionaries found it in the early 1800's and recorded it for posterity.

This very informal little tale-telling scene was drawn by the distinguished French artist Jacques Boullaire, who has lived many years off and on in the islands. Originally his illustrations and decorations that are scattered through these pages were done for a children's book of mine, an adaptation of Polynesian myths called *Tales of Maui*. The drawings, as you can readily see, are not at all juvenile, and with Monsieur Boullaire's kind permission I have reintroduced many of them here.

The Polynesians fashioned the epics of their race in a form which is usually called chants. They were partly sung, partly recited, sometimes partly danced. Led by the taua the chants were at times joined in by the audience, as chorus. The taua had learned the words by heart from their predecessors. On pain of death the taua had to be letter perfect in rendering the texts, despite their very great length. They probably took hours to recite. For a present-day reader the chants are tedious going, full of repetition and full to overflowing with names: names of gods, of people, of mountains and valleys and streams—even individual rocks were given names, sometimes compound ones, as distinctive as the names given children or chieftains. Another characteristic was an almost endless specification of rather obvious detail. It must be remembered that although these redundancies are wearisome to read on a printed page, when chanted or sung to a strong rhythm, with rising and falling cadences and emphases they can become varied and exciting. Since we cannot sing them here, perhaps the best way to convey the flavor of these chants is to give a few samples of their style and character, and then to summarize their narrative content. This, for instance, is a very short example of rhythmic repetition from a chant about the Chaotic Period, when Taaroa was creating the world.

"There was extension of Tumu Nui
There was extension of Paparaharaha
Extension of the chambers for the gods and man
And extension of the horizon, the sky was extended
It was widened with the pillars of the land of Havai'i.

Hades grew, and darkness extended
Mountains grew, and they multiplied
Water grew, and rushed on
The ocean grew and rolled forth
Rocks grew and increased
The skies grew and extended until they were ten in number
Rain developed and fell everywhere
Moss and slime grew and increased
Forests grew and increased
Food grew and increased
Paper mulberry grew and increased
Creeping plants grew and increased
Weeds grew and increased
Life quickened in the sea, in the rivers, and on the land
Living things grew in the sea, in the rivers, and on the land, and they increased in the sea, in the rivers, and on the land.

Taaroa looked below
And then he looked above
And he laughed on seeing what was revealed to him
When Taaroa saw all
He applauded
Earth had become land
And it was filled with living creatures
Fresh water flowed throughout the land
Sea filled the oceans, and they were filled with living creatures
But all was still in the thick darkness of the close sky of Rumia.

In Havai'i, the birthplace of land
Havai'i, the birthplace of gods
Havai'i, the birthplace of kings
Havai'i, the birthplace of man."

An instance that illustrates profuse naming is taken from another chant. It is a revelation, also, of the Polynesian's intimate knowledge of the stars. He had individual names for about two hundred stars, but recognized many more than that as associates of the principal ones, much as we give Greek letters to the stars in our constellations.

"The pillars of the sky, Rumia, have become great twinkling stars in the heavens
Anamua (Antares in Scorpio) is the entrance pillar of the sky that is Anahoa
Anamuri, weeping for Rio, god of bonito and albacore fishers (Aldebaran in Taurus), is the pillar to blacken or tattoo by
Anaroto (Spica in Virgo), is the pillar of perfect purity
Anatipu (Dubhe in Ursa Major), is the upper side pillar, the pillar to guard by
Anaheuheupo, throwing off darkness (Alphard, or Cor Hydra), a red star that flies in the open south, is the lower pillar, the pillar to debate by
Anatahu'a a ta'ata metua te tupu mavae, the fatherly priest of man who grew in space (Arcturus in Boötes), is the pillar to stand by
Anatahu'a vahine o toa te manava, the priestess of brave heart (Procyon in Canis Major), the pillar for elocution
Anavaru (Betelgeuse in Orion), the pillar to sit by
Anaiva (Phaet in Columba), the pillar of exit
Anania (Polaris or North Star in the Little Bear), is the pillar to fish by in the boundary of the sky."

Another example, showing the use of profuse detail is found in still another chant in which Taaroa creates his first god, Tane, "the child". Although definitely inferior to his father (indeed Tane was the first creation of a lower category of gods, because Taaroa was himself the top rank and the only one in it), Tane became his father's favorite and most frequent companion. In the various island groups, he had various attributes: god of the forests, of beauty, of rain, of the sea, of growth and life. Here is only a small section of the list of the stages of Tane's creation, perhaps one-fifteenth of the whole, a chronicle which starts with his skin and ends with all the various apertures, "bored with gimlet shells." And even the published version has undoubtedly been expurgated of many details which were particularly and unashamedly relished by the Polynesians (omitted perhaps because of Miss Henry's Victorian delicacy and perhaps also because of Reverend Orsmond's scruples).

"Then were set joints for the jaws
There were set cheeks, smooth cheeks, cheeks full of rage, flushed cheeks, wide, long cheeks for the child
There were set lips, pliant lips, pouting lips, laughing lips, sneering thick lips
And there were set the upper jaw and the lower jaw, and rows of teeth, teeth for the child to eat with
The exterior is set as a head for the child, now let there be set fullness for the head.

Then the skull of the head got filled with brain
Now set a tongue, a clamorous tongue, a voluble tongue, a licking tongue for the child, that the mouth may be perfect to talk with and to eat with
And set a knotty gullet and a slender throat, for a neck for the child
Let there be set shoulders formed so as to rest against pillows in sleeping for the child
And set arms, and odoriferous arm-pits, elbows, wrists and palms to the hands, fingers, and finger nails for the child
Let there be a broad chest, a flat bosom, ribs wide apart, a jointed spine, and a flexible back for the child.

Arise Atea, thou and establish!
Let there be set a throbbing heart, a swinging liver, swinging lungs, a stomach as a receptacle for food, a smilt, a caul, and kidneys for the child
Set large intestines, set small, curling intestines
These were the child's vitals, vitals containing a conscience

Symbolically the vitals meant to a Polynesian what the heart means to us, the seat of the emotions. To quote Davies's dictionary: "Aau, the bowels or intestines—*fig.* the heart or mind; the affections; the conscience; courage or spirit."

Let there be set a folding abdomen, with a deep
rounded umbilicus, comely loins and parted buttocks
Now set hollow groins, and shining limber thighs; set
knees, they must be bending knees
Let there be shin bones, for the legs of the child and
turned out feet, and toes with toe nails to push off
with for the child
Let the development of the child all be perfect
And now cover the child with a sleek, brown skin
And set little hairs by all the pores of the skin.

When this was done, the mind of Atea was set at rest
Then Atea stood up, took her basket of gimlet shells
under her arm, and bored into the round skull of the
child
She bored into the ears to listen by, and placed wax in
them
She bored into the nose and the talkative mouth and the
throat of the child
The child then moved, he wept, and cried
'O Atea, I am in great pain.'

Thus the development of the child was perfected,
accomplished it all
The child became a living being, it was the spirit of
Taaroa that directed the work, and caused
Tanematamorari (Tane of shapeless face) to become a
good looking boy
None of the artisans touched Tane, they were all afraid
of the majesty, the power of Atea."

Opposite
There is no good representation of Tane from Raiatea, so I shall borrow from one of the Cook islands, Rarotonga. These southern Polynesians were superb wood carvers and their artists were probably often imported to the Tahitian archipelago. Connoisseurs of Polynesian art give little aesthetic credit to our Society islanders because much more sophisticated and refined sculpture in both wood and stone has been found elsewhere—in Hawaii, New Zealand, Easter Island, the Marquesas, and in the scattered southern groups of the Cooks, Australs, Gambiers. Even a tiny outlying atoll like Nukuoro produced astonishing figures compared to the relatively crude ones of Tahiti whose talents, though outstanding, were apparently more social and poetical. But Danielsson has recently suggested that because the Tahitian islands were proselytized so early, much fine art may have been burned by the missionaries and thus did not survive for our appraisal.

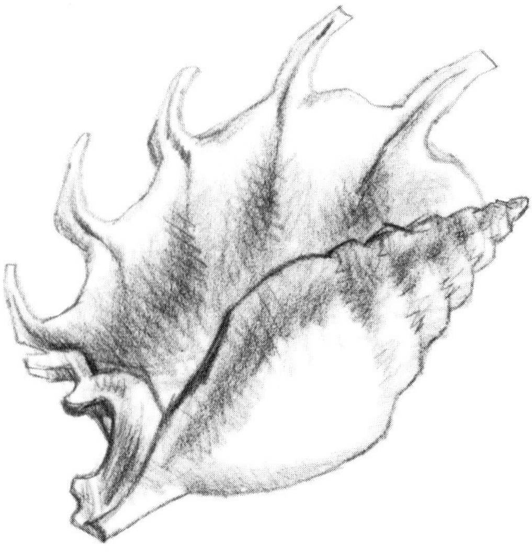

Here again we must borrow from Rarotonga for a carved image of Taaroa. This particular one is roughly done. There are many others as exquisitely wrought as Tane, such as the one opposite, but they are all broken at about a quarter of their length. (It was more practical to stow only the finely carved section on an old-time sailing ship. Why bother with the rest of a 13–15 foot staff?) I believe that this image in the British Museum is the only one that survives in full length, from serene head to sharply pointed penis. It signifies the splendid tradition of the male principle wrapped in the female bundle, an ancient one that echoes back to Polynesian origins in Indonesia.

Even after three such minute samples (the whole creation chant and its appendages must run several thousand lines) you may perhaps understand the contrasting comments of John Orsmond and his granddaughter, Teuira Henry. Writes he in his Preface, dated 1848:

"Feeling the great importance of crystallizing Tahitian literature in all its original simplicity and style of rendering, wherein lies its greatest charm, I have carefully collected the records as they fell from the lips of priests and bards and other learned natives of both sexes, in doing which, with pencil and paper in hand, I have been struck with the beauty of the language and the richness of many of the words and figures of speech. This folklore I have carefully revised with the aid of the best native scholars of all classes."

Later on Teuira (she died in 1915) states she is submitting for publication only small portions of the vast amount of material amassed by her grandfather, and that she has done a good deal of selecting and editing, moreover, because she considers it too tedious and repetitious for present-day readers. And, as already noted, we may suspect that in her eyes the texts were also probably too obscene. But the Polynesian evidently loved these chants —and the longer the better. Perhaps they are much easier and more pleasant to hear than to read. Perhaps too, the Polynesian had so much time on his hands that listening

At left is a figure from Tahiti reported to be "Tangaroa," but I have my doubts. He is hollow and his back is removable so he was thought to be filled with toy progeny gods as well as sprouting them from his body. Since this concept does not occur in the myths, he seems more a gimmick than a god.

to chants was an agreeable way to spend it. Most likely, I think, he took a lot more interest in his vivid ancestral gods and their wildly improbable exploits than could be expected of us.

"He was there · Taaroa was his name
All about him was emptiness
No where the land · No where the sky
No where the sea · No where man
Taaroa called out · No echo to answer.

Then in this solitude he became the world
This knot of roots it is Taaroa
The rocks are he again
Taaroa · The song of the sea
Taaroa · He named himself
Taaroa · Transparence
Taaroa · Eternity
Taaroa · The powerful
Creator of the universe which is but the shell of Taaroa
Who bestows on it life in beautiful harmony."

It is a great pity the Polynesians never evolved a Homer, because their chants and legends are wonderfully rich material, as distinctive as Greek epics, Norse sagas, or Indian Vedas and puranas. The creation chants tell how Taaroa lay in the darkness of his shell for countless ages. Nothing existed outside this shell—and even the nothingness is specified (no light, no noise, no sea, etc., etc.) at such length that the ages do indeed seem countless.

Eventually even the great Taaroa becomes weary of inaction and begins to stir. The shell cracks and, at length, he pushes it apart so that its upper half becomes the dome of the sky. Then he converts the lower portion into the Great Foundation Rock, Tumunui, which stands in utter darkness far down in a crevice of the extinct crater of the Temehani, by a great rushing stream of water called Vaitupo. Next, he commences the very long process of manufacturing the other gods, first Tane and then other descendants, including Rongo, Oro (god of war), Tu (stability), and Atea (vast expanse).* The list is bounteous and it is also confusing, because in the different island groups, such as the Tuamotus, Cooks, Australs, Hawaii, New Zealand, the various gods were given different attributes and different degrees of importance. (Even Tangaroa, the almighty, becomes only the god of the sea in Mangaia.) But it is a notable fact that in spite of all this confusion of function and rank, the same names are used throughout the distant island groups.

The secondary gods set about the housekeeping jobs of tidying up the universe. They prop up the heavens, create the stars, cover the earth with water, then raise up various islands. Most importantly, one or another of the gods fashions man and woman and sets them to propagating, while still others are clothing the mountains with forests, filling the seas with fish, calling forth all the various winds, and so on. Many of the final tasks, such as fetching fire and fishing up further islands, were left to demigods like Maui, for the members of the Polynesian pantheon, like those of their Greek contemporaries, did a good deal of consorting with humans—in the olden days, that is. There were many of these demi-gods, Hiro (patron of thieves), Hiro (the master canoe builder), Uahenga (tatu artist), Tafai (the overseas adventurer). But by far the most widely known and most popular of all was Maui, about whom, from the mythologist's point of view, perhaps the most remarkable thing was his ubiquity. Mauitikitiki was his full name and he is found not only in the folklore of all

Opposite
This drawing was made in 1869 and published in the *Journal of the Polynesian Society* by J. L. Young to illustrate a description by an old wiseman of the Tuamotus (tuhunga) of how his people thought of the creation of the world. Although the Tuamotus lie several hundred miles northeast of Raiatea, the concept is common throughout Polynesia. The Tuamotus had nine layers or spheres of the heavens: the Maoris had twelve, but most other Polynesians, including the Raiateans, had eight. Eight was the most common multiple in the islands, comparable perhaps to our ten. Our ten is generally believed to be derived from our digits: their eight perhaps from the fingers alone.

* Atea was usually female, and, fertilized by Taaroa, was the begettress of most of the other gods.

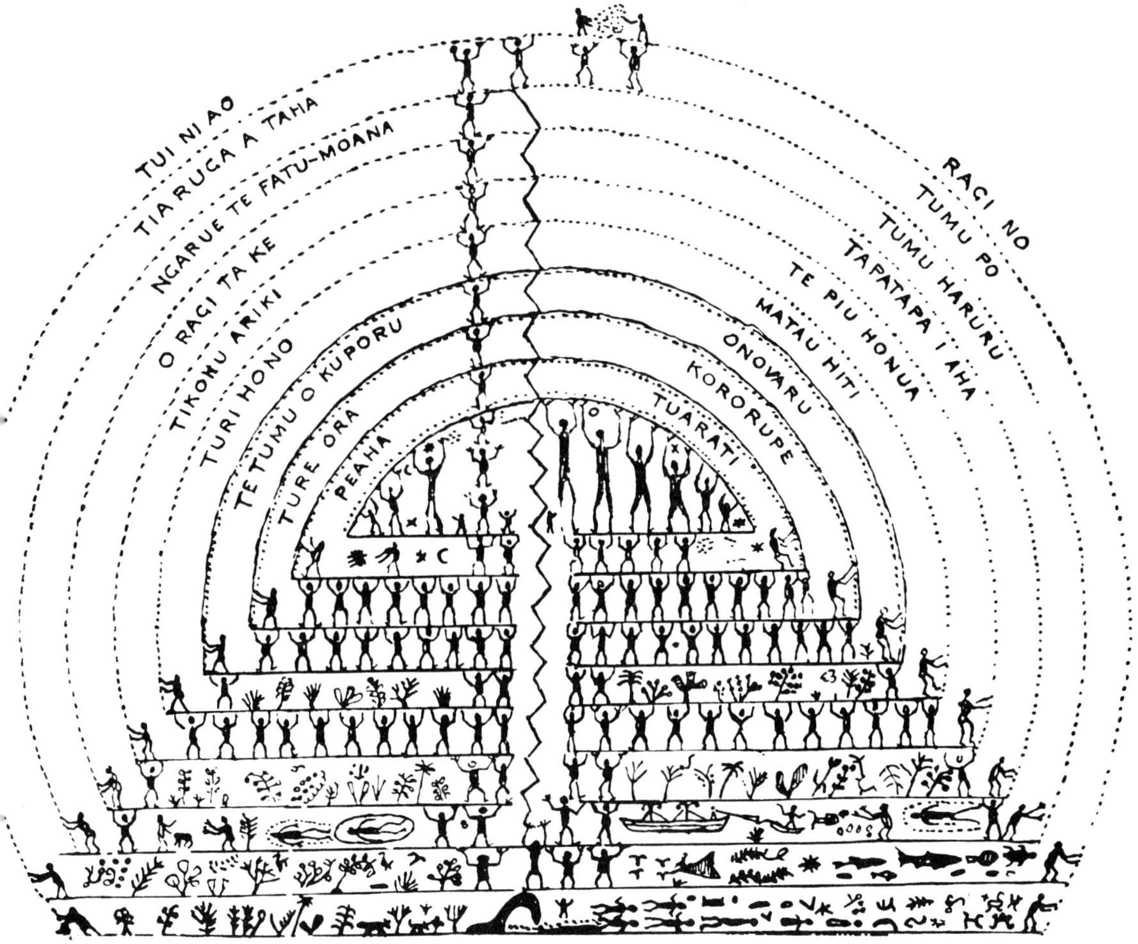

the Polynesian islands, he was widely known, too, in many areas of Micronesia and Melanesia as well. I believe he is the only oceanic hero who covers so much territory.

Maui's story is interesting. He was of course born in Raiatea, and his birth was a strange one: early embryonic, or what we might call a miscarriage or possibly an abortion. His mother, Huahenga, wrapped him in the magic hairs from the top of her head and tossed him out to sea. The little bundle floated in the hot sun, and the birds fed the child as they would one of their own. (Maui's best friends and companions throughout his life were birds, and there may also be psychological implications here, for Moana, the sea, is the mother of all life.) Finally, Maui grew into a handsome boy. He had some difficulty being recognized by his family and accepted into it, largely because he had four older brothers who had little use for him. But eventually he became his mother's favorite. This

Teuira Henry says, "After the skys were disposed of, the people who were at that time immortal and endowed with great power, created the stars to illuminate the highest heavens, the sun to shine lower down and the moon nearest the earth. All these celestial bodies rose up through shafts in their horizons in the east, and set through others in corresponding horizons in the west, all in regular succession except the sun, which caused the days and nights to be irregular." Diagrammatically quaint perhaps, but astronomically sharp enough.

alienated the brothers still more, but it gave Maui magical powers, because his mother was a goddess.

As he grew up he became a great trickster and boaster, traits always favored in Polynesia, provided they can be carried off with humor. Soon he embarked on his famous deeds. These, like those of Hercules, are so widely known that I will simply list a few of the more famous here:

1) Maui set out to find the dwelling place of his parents during the day (for Huahenga slept with her sons at night), and this he did by changing himself into a pigeon and flying down through underground caverns to paradise.

2) Maui felt a need for a magic weapon, and by flattery and guile he succeeded in obtaining the jawbone of the blind, cannibal goddess, Ranganua, an ancestress of his, one side of whose body was alive, the other side dead, thus representing the transition zone so important to Polynesians.

3) In those days the sun went so fast across the sky

that there was not time for the people to cook their meals properly. So with the help of his brothers Maui made a huge net, snared the sun, and beat it with his magic jawbone until it promised to go more slowly—as it still does to this day. (This sun snaring is a puzzler to mythologists because it occurs in several other totally unrelated cultures.)

4) Perhaps Maui's best-known and most spectacular feat was fishing up islands from the bottom of the sea. He made a great fishhook (of which there must be a hundred in the museums of the world) and baited it with the lobe of his left ear.

5) He brought fire to the earth by persuading the goddess of fire, who dwells in a smoking volcanic crater, to pluck out her fingernails and toenails. At her last big toe she suspects Maui of trickery. A great crisis ensues. The whole earth is in flames and Maui almost dead when Taaroa at last sends torrential rains. Some of the fire escaped to certain trees, and by rubbing their woods together man has made fire ever since.

6) There are many other such legends and many variations in the different groups, but I will summarize further only the last:

When Maui noticed gray hairs on his mother's head, he asked what they meant and she told him she was growing old and would soon die. Maui was sad and he determined to conquer Nuitepo, the great goddess of death. To do this he would have to work his way up into the aperture through which he was born and come out of her mouth. He was warned that this was extremely dangerous, but he set out one night to the region of the sky where the old goddess lived. Warning his companions, the little birds, that they must never make the slightest noise, he stripped himself naked and was working his way up, up, up. But when his head came out of the goddess's mouth, the little wandering tattler burst out laughing. This woke the goddess up, and she snapped off Maui's head and swallowed his body. According to the traditions of the Polynesians, this final feat of Maui was the last chance for the people of this world to escape death and to live forever.

And now for a more detailed accounting of one of Maui's exploits which has particular pertinence to Raiatea. The story is typical of the legends, and it happens to be one of my favorites.*

* This is an adaptation from many sources as it was printed in my book, *Tales of Maui.*

Te Tuna

In the dark cold depths of the sea lived the giant eel, Te Tuna, who carried in his head the seed of life. And with him dwelt a beautiful maiden named Hina. Te Tuna had a longing for this girl and wished to make her his wife, but Hina was afraid of the great eel. She found no pleasure in his dark gloomy house, she did not want to touch his slimy skin, and she was afraid that he might enter her and bite inside her. And so whenever Te Tuna came close to her, she would flee to the earth above, to the sunshine and the company of mankind to seek a hero who would deliver her from the great eel. But in spite of her beauty, her soft-singing voice, her graceful dancing, and her sweet-smelling skin she could find no one brave enough to contest the magic of the eel who always brought her back from the sunny world to his shivery black cave in the depths of the sea.

Then one day Te Tuna said to her, "I have noticed you going away from me many times. Always I have to fetch you back again, and each time you give me some excuse, that you are sick or that you must visit your parents. So I have decided that I will shut you up in my house and keep you with me always."

Hina was very frightened when the great eel said this, and she answered him, "Very well, if you say, it must be so, but first let me make the far journey to the great marae of Taputapuatea at Opoa on the island of Havaiki, for that is the most sacred place in all the world, and there I will commit myself to the gods and prepare myself."

Te Tuna was very angry and he threshed about in his cave so that great tidal waves swept across the waters, but his magic was not strong enough to contest the power of the most ancient gods, so he let Hina go, telling her that she would know when she must return, for at that time by the sweep of his long tail he would send a wave so massive that it would surge right to the altar of Taputapuatea and summon her back to him.

Hina then traveled to Havaiki many, many leagues over the slippery ooze of the ocean floor. When she arrived, the first thing she sought was a freshwater pool in a mountain stream so she could bathe and refresh herself. While she was splashing about in the delicious cool water, Maui chanced to come near and saw her through the thick leaves.

"Oho!" he said to himself softly. "What is this?" He watched for a while and saw that the girl was very beautiful. Then he climbed into a tree, hid himself on a low branch, and plucked a white pua flower and threw it into the pool in front of her. Hina was much pleased that such a lovely flower had fallen. She picked it up and put it behind her ear. After a while Maui tossed another flower, and again Hina pounced on it with delight and looked up to see where it had fallen from. Then Maui took still a third flower, but this time before tossing it to her, he nib-

bled off the tips of the petals with his teeth. When she picked it up, she at last realized that these flowers had not dropped by chance, but had been thrown by some person. She was frightened at this, but she was also curious about what sort of person would throw her such sweet-scented flowers.

Then Maui stood up on the branch and made a long dive out of the tree into the pool beside her. After they had played for a while in the water, he took her and brought her to his house and asked his brothers and their wives to make room for her. They saw how beautiful was this maiden that Tikitiki had found, and they made a place for her on their sleeping mats.

And Hina was happy and forgot the great eel until one night a vast wave swept over the reef from the southward and rushed into the house of Maui and beyond, even to the altar of Taputapuatea.

Maui was angry to be awakened from his peaceful sleep by the cold water, and he shouted out, "Who has dared to throw this challenge at Mauitikitiki a Huahenga?"

Then Hina told him of Te Tuna and of how she must now return to him, and she wept and she wept. Maui then seized the jawbone of Ranganua from its resting place up near the rafters of his house, where it was accustomed to hang with the relics of his ancestors, and he went out on the reef to the edge of the Great Ocean and shouted a challenge at Te Tuna, daring him to come fight for the maiden.

The eel heard the challenge in his cavern beneath the cold waters of the southern ocean, and he hastened over the sea to contest with Maui. On the way he asked many people what sort of warrior this Maui was.

"Is he very large?"

"Oh, no," they told him, "he is not nearly so big as you are, but he is quick and strong and he has great magic and may play tricks on you."

"Well, my magic is powerful, too; you shall see. And if he is a small fellow, I will surely conquer him."

As he approached Havaiki, Te Tuna prepared three great waves to overwhelm Maui as he stood on the reef. The first wave was not very large, and Maui easily withstood it and laughed defiantly at the eel as it crashed by. Then the second wave came, and it rose up with great force and hurled itself at Maui, but he clung fast to the sacred stone he had brought with him from his temple. At last the wave passed and he was still there.

He stood the sacred block of pink coral on its end and said to it, "When the third one comes, you must run on up the beach ahead of the wave as fast as you can."

The third wave began to swell up above him, and it was so huge that it darkened the whole sky and filled the land with the roar of its waters. And on its black back rode Te Tuna, ready to kill Maui. But when he saw the sacred stone running for the beach in all the turmoil of the lashing spray, he mistook it for his victim and swam swiftly, way up onto the land into the sloping valley of Opoa in pursuit of it. So when the wave receded, there he lay stranded, and Maui came and with a mighty blow of his enchanted weapon cut off the head of the great eel.

Te Tuna, seeing he was defeated at last, told Maui that he should bury his head in a sacred place and bring fresh water every day to moisten that ground. After some weeks a tree would grow and he should care for it and let no one cut it down because from it would come a lasting benefit to mankind.

And it was thus that Maui brought the coconut to the people of the earth, for it sprouted from the head of the great eel, Te Tuna. To them it brought more wealth than any of their other trees. Its trunk made sturdy posts for their houses. From its wood they carved many of their sacred idols. Its young leaves made gaily woven hats to keep the hot sun away. Its huge fronds became the symbol of peace for the people of the islands. The leaflets of these fronds were interlaced to make thatch for their roofs and mats for their walls. Its meshed fibers made sieves and nets and, when unraveled, were braided into strong ropes and lashings. A delicious wine was gathered from the tip of the tender central spathe. The husks of the nuts kindled the first sparks and made the hottest cooking fires. The shells of the nuts, cut in halves, made drinking cups and eating bowls and even canoe bailers. The meat of the nut, when young, was a sweet, nourishing jelly; when older, it was grated and squeezed to make the sauce they liked so well, and when old and dried in the sun, it gave forth the sweet-smelling oil with which they loved to rub their skin. The liquid in the tender nuts was always pure and refreshing to drink, and on some low coral atolls was at times the only source of drinking water. Even the bark and the roots gave valuable medicines.

Thus many blessings came from this famous tree, and you will still see even today, at the crown of the nut, the three dark places that were left from the two eyes and the mouth of the giant eel.

Out of all this and the works of other gods, the whole tapestry of Polynesian ideas and beliefs was woven—a tapestry as complete as our Genesis, but it took a lot longer than six days. The result argues for a common or central origin of Polynesian culture. And since Taaroa started the world and made his residence in the great crater of the Temehani, the suggestion of this book is that the origin was Raiatea. Not the origin of the race, for that was clearly southeast Asia, and even Raiaitea was not peopled until many centuries of settlement had passed in the Samoa-Tonga-Fiji complex.

L. M. Groube recently expressed very well what most Polynesian scholars seem increasingly to be believing. "The Polynesians," he says, "did not strictly come from anywhere: they *became* Polynesian and the location of their becoming was Tonga." My supposition, based largely on personality and partly on physique, is that Raiatea was settled from Samoa and became their holy land. There the culture (as distinct from the race, if one can distinguish between the two) acquired its final individuality, and from there it radiated to the outlying groups: the Cooks, Australs, Gambiers, Easter, Hawaii, New Zealand. Of course in saying that it radiated from Raiatea, the whole of central Polynesia is meant: the Societies, Tuamotus, Marquesas. From a point of view of acreage, Raiatea is an insignificant island in this central Pacific assemblage. Its significance lies in the fact that it was chosen to be the focal point of the religious beliefs of the Polynesians, and thus the fountain-head of their spiritual culture.

This theory assumes that, after settlement from Samoa, the Polynesians consolidated and refined their culture in the central Pacific over a long period of time, several centuries at least, and then sent it forth in all directions—back westward to the "outliers," and even back to where they came from in Tonga-Samoa-Fiji; proselitizing their parents so to speak.

CHAPTER FIVE

The Sacred Mountain

The Temehani, its highest point 772 meters, is not the highest mountain in Raiatea. The loftiest is Te Mou'a, "La Sainte," (1,017 meters), that dominates the sacred village of Opoa and its huge marae, Taputapuatea. Tepatuarahi is 945 meters. These two adjacent mountains are the dwelling places of the gods, whereas the Temehani is the gathering place and dispatching station for mortal souls.

The Temehani has a very large and very irregular base, an extensive high plateau and twin peaks, Temehani Rahi or Great Temehani and Temehani Ute Ute or Red Temehani. There are two shoulders of the Temehani on both of which the flower grows. One is on the central and eastern slopes, just north of the mountain's highest point. The other, further north, might almost be called a separate mountain, because of the dip in altitude between them, but it is unquestionably the same mountain mass and the whole of it has always been called the Mehani by the natives. Mehani, according to Teuira Henry, means heat or the heat. She writes that, "The Tahitians were familiar with volcanic workings from their knowledge of Hawaii and other lands, but they have no record of active volcanoes existing in their own group. The name Mehani . . . meaning 'heat' is evidently a traditional way of accounting for its origin." I doubt she is right about Hawaii, because this would mean that the Mehani was not so named until after Hawaii's discovery, many hundreds of years after the discovery of Raiatea. More likely the proto-Polynesians brought this knowledge with them from their more distant migrations through Melanesia. Certainly they had been exposed to volcanoes and it would be characteristic of them to remember such spectacular phenomena even over a millenium or two.

A view from the "plateau" of the Temehani with the two motus that mark the entrance to the harbor of Uturoa. The barrier reef beyond the blue lagoon runs away from them roughly north and south. Beyond the reef lies the ocean and, on a clear day, one can see the silhouette of the neighboring island of Huahine on the horizon.

On the northwestern shoulder of the Temehani is the Apoonui or "Great Hole," famed in legend as the place where the spirits of the dead are sorted out by a kind of Polynesian Cerberus named Romatane. Those who have not paid sufficient attention to the rites of the marae are directed down the hole. The devout are waved westward to Havaiki. The legends are somewhat confusing, because they were probably never very precise, as is the way with legends, and furthermore they were first recorded by missionaries, and missionaries, especially in those days, had a tendency to give the native "religion" Biblical twists. Here at the Hole the parallel of Heaven and Hell and even of Purgatory was apparently irresistable. Later on, the early sectarian scholars sensed parallels in Greek mythology. So just what these people believed is recorded one way by one group and another way by another, with many variations in imagination and conviction amongst the individuals in the groups. If only those early missionaries had had tape recorders! Now, not only are the old taua or sages long since gone, but even their archaic language is

Another view of the same two islets from another part of the mountain as we were on our way up.

largely incomprehensible to their present-day descendants.

I shall choose, as the best recourse, to select from various sources the versions that seem most characteristically Polynesian. This is admittedly an unscientific procedure because it depends on hunch and feel derived from personal association with present-day Polynesians. I happen to believe that their basic personality traits are fortunately consistent with those of their ancestors, that in a race as strongly individualistic as the Polynesians their fundamental attitudes and attributes have not succumbed, as their superficial ones have, to the European take-over. This may lead us into illusions, but I hope you will find them to be interesting ones, however unscientific they may perhaps be.

The Hole itself is real enough, three or four meters wide: eight or ten meters long and about twice as deep as it is long or "at least 16 meters," as recorded by the Whitney Expedition in 1922. (Ten feet by thirty feet by fifty deep is roomy enough to hold quite a few disembodied spirits, especially since they apparently did not always

These two extraordinary pictures of the famous "Hole," also the one from the plateau, and still two others in the color section, were taken by Michel Liaut, a genial merchant of Uturoa whose camera hobby has made him, in my opinion, the outstanding resident photographer of the island.

stay there indefinitely. Purgatory?) A more specific description was made by Edward T. Perkins in 1854. With two companions he ascended through Tepua Valley, which faces the historic Teavarua Harbor on the eastern side of Raiatea. He describes the place as follows:

"After passing several small streams, some of which had worn deep channels in the rock, we reached the vicinity of the cave. The side of the mountain seemed one mass of porous rock (volcanic) scantily covered with creeping vegetation . . .

"The famous cave was apparently nothing more than a deep fissure in the rock about 30 feet long, 15 broad and 80 feet deep by measurement. A small stream that had worn a deep channel shot over the ledge at its upper extremity, and fell in a shower upon the loose shingle at the bottom. The most favorable point for observation is from the lower side, or towards the sea; but owing to its depth and jutting points, a small portion only of the bed is discernible."

A rope was let down, and Mr. Perkins descended to the

lowest part, 80 feet below. He goes on to say:

"The area of the bottom was considerably greater than that of the mouth, owing to the receding of the sides. These were basaltic, and for about 30 feet consisted of massive boulders piled up in curvilinear rows, and partaking of the trappean formation."

At the upper end a dark passage led downwards, and with a torch he commenced the descent. He continues:

"No stronger evidence of the volcanic origin of the island would be required than the appearance of this fissure, which was in every respect similar to those noticed in the immediate vicinity of Kilauea, with the exception that the others bore traces of more recent igneous action. The cavern consisted of a number of low, irregular passages, branching out in various directions and inclining seaward, with a rapid or abrupt descent. I took the principal one, sometimes walking, and again crouching almost to the earth, until it terminated in a chasm . . . I found it was but little more than 10 feet deep, after which there was a continuation of the gloomy vault; the descent was easy by the irregularity of the sides. But here the path was obstructed by massive rocks . . . I groped along, making another descent similar to the first. Since entering this subterranean vault, I had heard a faint sound as of water percolating among loose rocks, which as I advanced gradually increased, until now it seemed rushing above and around while its roaring through the narrow passages was almost deafening. The atmosphere was damp and chilling."

* * *

The spirits of the dead were very real to the Polynesian and their doings of utmost importance to him. Their first procedure on their way to the hereafter was to assemble before three rocks named Ofaiarariorio (Rock that is the veiller of the spirit), Ofaimaueraa (Rock that takes the spirit by the nape of the neck). Ofaireiriorio (Rock that sets the spirit in flight). From these they mounted the Temehani. There they were separated and dispatched in accordance with their respective merits.

Another version has them gathering first of all before two rocks at Papeari in Moorea, although these perhaps are the spirits from Tahiti, rather than Raiatea. Here the stones are Ofaiora (Rock of life) and Ofaipohe (Rock of death). Souls touch the stones by hazard, because they are blind. If one encounters the stone of life it commences its migration, the first stage of which is a sojourn on the Temehani, followed by a departure for the islet of Tupai or Motuiti on the northwest coast of Bora Bora, and thence presumably to the legendary Havaiki in the west. If, however, the soul blunders into the stone of death it may just flutter about. Souls are uneasy and they like to torment the living. These unguided ones are the famous

Opposite
It may seem that I am reaching far afield or far aloft for illustration in using a number of the works of Paul Gauguin, but why cannot one look to a painter on the spot as valid in the role of reporter as an explorer, a missionary, or an anthropologist? Gauguin was fascinated by Tahitian mythology and culture. His "reporting" may not be meticulously scientific (as was that of Cook's artists, Parkinson, Hodges, and Webber), indeed it it is often factually sloppy, but it always has a spirit which tunes truly with the themes of this book. Unfortunately he never visited the island of Raiatea, but he painted many of its characteristics and emanations. I like to see his *Death Watch* as depicting Hina in that breathless interval between her death and the return of Tafai when her spirit took flight for the Temehani.

or, rather, infamous tupapau that frighten you in the dark and might steal the skull of your ancestor from the eaves of your house while you sleep. Often they pass into the bodies of sea birds and fly about crying at night. Still another belief has them sojourn on the highest mountain of Raiatea, Te moua moa.

This visit in Po (Darkness or Death) is divided, on the one hand, into a sort of purgatory for sinful souls and, on the other, a place where souls dance an eternal upa upa under the guard of the god Urataetae. At the gate (Is this perhaps the Great Hole?) is a god called Romatane, who has the power to admit or exclude. Certain souls, perhaps those who have been excluded from the paradise of Rohutu, transform themselves into malevolent, inferior gods, the Oromatua, who conjure up evil. Two sorts of Oromatua are especially fearsome, the "eaters of old folk" and the "long toothed Oromatua" who return to strangle and devour their surviving parents.

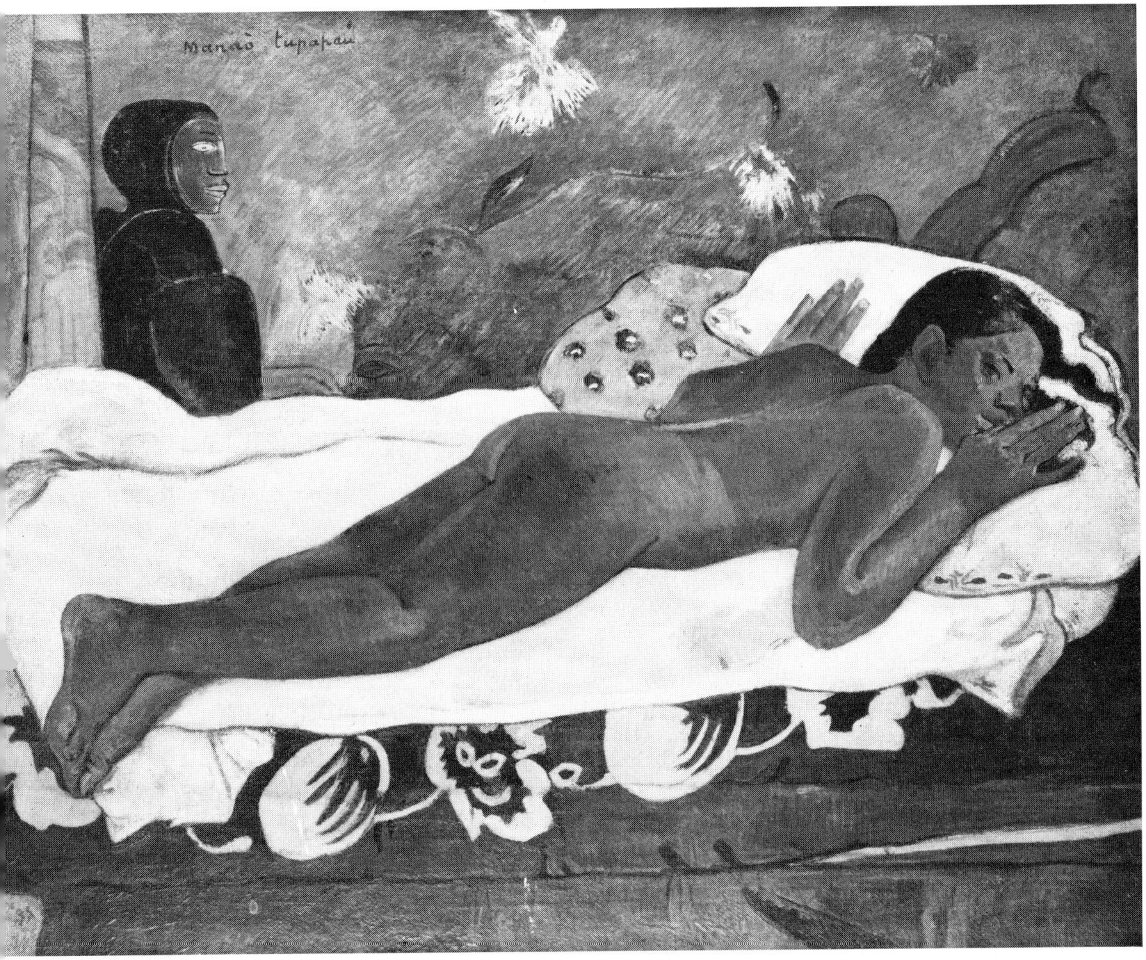

Tafai's famous canoe, *Niu*, was an outrigger even though it made many an heroic voyage to the outskirts of the Polynesian world, climbed mountains and descended cavernous vortexes. It may have looked something like this one painted by Lieutenant Tobin, who was Bligh's second-in-command. Kenneth Emory has pronounced this the best representation of a typical Tahitian-type sailing, outrigger canoe.

Scraps from the Legend of Tafai give us a more intimate experience with the Temehani. Here it is; condensed and occasionally quoted from Teuira Henry:

Tafai was a folk hero, second only to Maui in renown and almost as widespread over the ocean. His exploits were recounted by the New Zealand Maori as Tawaki, by the Hawaiians as Kahai, but it was Tafai in most other island groups. He was known principally for his prowess as a seagoing adventurer. It was he who towed the Hawaiian islands into their present position and who, when sucked down into the sea by a huge whirlpool, was rescued by his magical alter ego, a huge blue-black shark that always watched out for him wherever he sailed.

Tafai was the second son of Hina, a powerful goddess who fell in love and married a mortal named Hema. Tafai was a giant blond child who was hairy like his grandfather, and from his earliest days it was evident that he possessed supernatural powers and was in touch with the gods. His older brother was simply an earthly chief, overshadowed by his mother, but the two played happily together and with their many cousins. Their favorite game was totoie or toy canoe. Each made his own canoe from the rib of a coconut leaf, rigged with a pandanus sail. The totoie were taken out in the sea, released, and raced to the shore. One day at his mother's suggestion, Tafai made his canoe from the stem of a gourd. This was much lighter than the others and easily won all the races. Whereupon all of Tafai's cousins became very angry. They ganged up on him and beat him until, as was the kindly way with boys in those days, they believed he was dead. So they buried him. But his mother, being a goddess, sensed that something was wrong and hastened to resuscitate him.

There he was the next day with his astonished cousins, as tall and strong as ever. And thus it went all through his youth. Although he was beaten to death many times, he was a kindly boy and never sought revenge. His father, Hema, however, was so chagrined by the cruelty of Tafai's playmates and cousins that he decided one afternoon (as Polynesians do even to this day) to leave this world of sin and strife and to go down to the darkness of Po, the afterlife.

When Tafai was still a youth his mother bestowed all her magical powers on him by having him open his mouth over the crown of Hina's head.

"At length Tafai reached man's estate. A great red man was he, modelled by the gods. He had bright curly auburn hair, his head and shoulders towered above all other tall men in Tahiti, he had penetrating brown eyes, his hands were large and strong, and his fingernails were long and pointed. Whenever he walked his majestic tread left footprints upon the most hardened ground. He became famous throughout the land for his wisdom and skill in all he did. Without tuition he excelled in every art of his time and his bravery and generosity won for him the respect and love of all in Tahiti, so that he was unanimously elected toa-upo'o-tu, chief warrior by all the warrior chiefs contemporary with him."

Tafai sets out upon many heroic ventures, most of them seagoing, but the incident in his life that concerns us here was his marriage to a beautiful young chiefess, famed for her raven black hair that flowed down in waves to her feet and covered her whole graceful and majestic form so that she needed no clothing. Her name was also Hina, which is a not uncommon name in Tahiti, because although it means, literally, gray, Hina was the goddess of the moon. It is perhaps comparable to our name Mary.

Tafai and Hina were very happy together, but they had not been married long when Tafai came back from one of his far-off voyages to find that Hina had died suddenly in his absence. Her body was still warm, lying in state on an altar in their ancestral marae. He asked the priests and elders where her spirit had flown and was told that it was on its way to the meeting place of spirits in Tahiti, and thence to Mount Rotui in Moorea, where it would take off for the Temehani in Raiatea. Tafai seized his great paddle and swiftly launched his magical canoe, Niu. He darted over the smooth water of the lagoon to Paea, arriving just at dusk the right time to meet departing souls. He found, however, that his wife's spirit had already left for Mount Rotui, so he sped across the channel and raced up the steep mountain into the clouds. But again he found that his lost Hina had gone on ahead of him. It was a long way to Raiatea, over the Sea of the Moon, more than 100 miles. Tafai had to use all the magic of his huge paddle and his slim canoe, but with a fair wind and the light of a waning moon, he sped to Raiatea and climbed swiftly up the Temehani to the place on the plateau of the mountain where the roads forked, one to the cliff on the right, called "The Stone of Life," from which spirits ascended to the "Paradise of Sweet Odor" somewhere up in the cloudland above the highest mountains of Raiatea, and the other to the cone on the left, where they descended down into the yawning crater which led to the Po.

The moon was almost setting and the morning star was heralding the day when Tafai arrived and was met by the god Tutahoroa, who guarded the roads. Tafai asked if Hina, his wife, had passed by, and to his great relief the god said she had not yet come. Then he told Tafai to hide

himself in the bushes* close by and to capture her in her flight, as this was the last place whence spirits could be recalled to this world. Breathlessly Tafai seated himself and soon he heard leaves rustling a little way off. The god told him to be ready, as Hina had just arrived.

"Soon Tafai perceived the tall, familiar form of his wife with her hair streaming down her back, and as she arrived on the ridge of the rock she drew back as she scented a human being. Just as she was about to ascend into the air to fly to the Stone of Life, where she would have escaped him, he made a desperate leap up onto the ledge and into the air and caught her by her flowing hair with his long

* These must surely have been the apetahi.

fingernails. Hina struggled to be released, since she was intent on going to the happy spirit world, but her husband held her fast, and when Tutahorea told her that her time had not yet come to leave this world, she was prevailed upon to remain longer with her husband. So they returned to Uporu, and as soon as Hina re-entered her body, which was well-preserved, and opened her mortal eyes, there was great rejoicing in their home and in all the district over the safe return of Tafai and his wife from the border of the spirit world.

"It is not recorded in Tahiti that Tafai ever again went away from his native land, but it is stated that he and his wife lived long and happy together and that of them was born a son whom they named Vahi-e-ro (Place-entirely-strange), probably in commemoration of the long voyages of Tafai to strange lands.

"In the manuscript dictionary by Mr. Orsmond, under the heading of the name Tafai, are found these words: *E atua Tafai-iri-ura, te turunu i Havaii, E mea navenave te 'a'ai o Tafai* (A god was Tafai of red skin, who raised up Havaii. Charming is the legend of Tafai). In Tahiti his memory is perpetuated in the form of the beautiful club moss (Licopodium clavatum) named *rimarima Tafai* (fingers of Tafai), which is said to have sprung from his fingers after he left his earthly body and which grows prolifically among the ferns over all the islands; the spores of the plant are called *mai 'u 'u Tafai* (fingernails of Tafai) which they are said to resemble."

A scrap from another legend may seem repetitious but it has intriguing variations. After a natural death the Polynesians believed that the spirit remained by the body three days before leaving it. From the body, the soul, warding off evil spirits with 'ura amulets, went to Puna'auia, the grand place of assemblage for all disembodied souls in Tahiti. If it alighted there upon the "Stone of Life," it could return by powerful attraction to its body; but if it went on to the "Stone of Death," it was forever cut off from its mortal remains. In either case it flew to Rotui in Moorea, and thence to Mount Temehani in Raiatea. At the crossroad stood the god Tutahoroa, and when the spirit coming from the Stone of Life met him he would under certain conditions tell it to return to its body to remain a while longer in this life. But generally he merely pointed to one of the two roads, which the spirit silently took. When allowed to go to the right, it flew on to meet Romatane (Voluptuous man), who received the ura feather amulets as peace offerings. Then the spirit was safely ushered into Paradise (Rohutu of Sweet Odor). But when directed to the left, the spirit had no choice but to obey and to fly down into the crater of the Temehani and be ushered into the presence of Ta'aroanuituhimate (Great Taaroa whose curse was death). In this region the rank of mortal beings was not respected, but all were treated alike. Kings, noblemen, and plebeians, according to their capabilities, were food gatherers, fishermen, planters, and menial servants to the gods. Queens and all classes of women served the goddesses, for, as the legends of old Tafai and the goddess Pere show, the same kinds of life were supposed to exist both above ground and below. When their work was done these captive spirits had to sit about in the region of utter darkness, by the ever-rushing river where Taaroa liked to dwell. When it pleased Taaroa, his cooks scraped the spirits into a pulp with a cockleshell, as sweetening for his taro-leaf spinach. But this process did not annihilate them, and they came again to be at Taaroa's disposal.

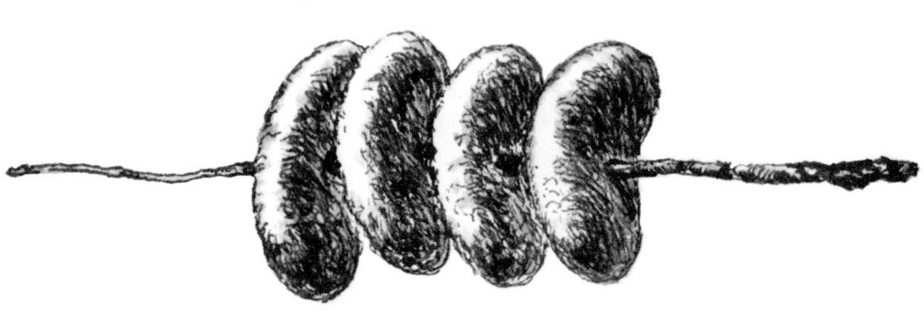

These then, were the essentials of the Polynesian's concept of the creation of his rocky land and its covering with vegetation and life. It is tempting to note one curious, though I am sure entirely coincidental, parallel in the two creations, one scientific, the other legendary. Tahiti was the "fish that swam away." It was originally part of the leeward cluster, but when a certain giant eel became enraged by the ill treatment and lack of respect he received from the people of Raiatea, he seized that land mass and carried it away to release it (a hundred or so miles to the eastward) where Tahiti is now situated. The first dorsal fin of the fish became Tahiti's great central mountain, Orohena, and the second dorsal fin, the island of Moorea. Geologically speaking Tahiti is actually of much more recent origin than Raiatea and her neighbors. (Of course, the Polynesian arrived far too late to observe this, perhaps several million years too late, but did he somehow sense it?) This difference in geological time might possibly be a clue as to why the tiare apetahi will not grow on Tahiti; perhaps the terrain, even at the proper altitude, is not yet mellow enough.

That Raiatea was once a much larger landmass is corroborated by another legend reported by the missionary John Williams in the early 1800's:

"In conversation with an old priest, who at that time was a decided and excellent Christian, respecting the situation of Rarotonga, he informed me that there was a tradition that it was formerly united to the southern extremity of Raiatea, but that the gods had carried it away. I asked him whither they were said to have conveyed it? when he replied, that he did not know, but it was believed they had taken it to the south. Upon this, I inquired the reason of the gods carrying away so valuable a neighbour as an island and its inhabitants? and he informed me that the natives of Rarotonga, in the exercise of their piety, had made a large drum, called *Tai-moana,* or the Sounder of the Seas, which they sent, by the hands of two priests, as a present to Oro, the god of war, whose residence was the great marae, at Opoa, in Raiatea, and that, after the priests from Rarotonga had dedicated *Tai-moana,* some untoward circumstance occurred, which induced the Raiateans to kill them. The gods were so much enraged that persons who had brought so valuable a present should be killed, that they took up the island, with its population, and carried it completely away. From some parts of this fabulous legend, we were convinced that the island was in existence, and that it was an island of considerable importance. From another tradition, which stated what was universally believed, we learned that a chief named Iouri, many years ago, built a large native *pahi,* or ship; and being a person of an enterprising spirit, he determined to go in search of other countries, when, after traversing the ocean for a length of time, he reached Rarotonga; from which place he returned safely to Raiatea, bringing with him a female, who became the wife of Tamatoa, the king of that island, and an ancestor of the late excellent chief of that name. From hence, also, Iouri brought a quantity

One of the most spectacular features of the "fish that swam away" is *la Diadème* in the central part of the island.

of *mahi,* or preserved breadfruit, which was dedicated to the god Oro, at the celebrated marae at Opoa, in Raiatea, the grand emporium of idolatry to Tahiti, the Society, and the surrounding islands; and from that time it became an object of ambition with every adventurous chief to discover other lands, and on his return to bring some article of value to his own land."

One wonders what that "untoward circumstance" could have been. Something the good Reverend might have found too Polynesian to mention? And note his characterization of Raiatea as the "grand emporium of idolatry," a confirmation in one sense perhaps of the island's importance.

Another legend reported by the eminent Pacific botanist E. J. Merrill, in 1954, carries the adventurers of our little island still further afield:

"He also gave me the outline of an almost forgotten

Raiatean legend regarding the discovery of South America by Maui Marumamao, including the route, the time spent in South America where Maui Marumamao died, the return of his son to Easter Island, and eventually, with at least some of the party to Raiatea. The route eastward was from Raiatea to Hikuveru (on maps, Hikueru), Marokakau (on some maps, Marokau) and Raroia, all in the Tuamotu group. From these islands he proceeded to Rapanui (Easter Island) and thence to 'Te Au Tuaivi, the land of ridges (or backbones), namely South America.'" Most of the anthropologists and ethnologists who have worked in the Polynesian field apparently did not learn of this legend. It offers no real evidence, but supplies as valid an argument as the legends covering the discovery and populating of New Zealand, including the introduction of the sweet potato there. What is perhaps most important is that this legend covers the sailing directions and includes the names of the foods which they took with them on the eastward voyage. One judges that there is here a much more logical explanation of the evidence regarding the American influence on Polynesian organizations and cultures than what he claimed. Such influence, in all fields, is much more apt to have been due to returned Polynesians, who had lived in the Inca dominated parts of South America for a considerable period of time, than by a few stray Indians cast ashore on a Polynesian island from a balsa raft!

A recently restored Easter Island *ahu* with its statue characteristically facing inland and its back to the sea. Archaeologist William Mulloy who, over the past few years, has been restoring the old statues, has discovered recently that many of them are astronomically oriented usually lining up the solstices or equinoxes.

Dr. Peter
July 17, 1929.

CHAPTER SIX

Seven or So Wonders of the Ancient World of Raiatea

Now that the creation of Raiatea is complete, we might give some attention to the ways of life of its people, before their spirits danced the upa upa* on high or served as sauce for Taaroa's spinach down below. Too much has been written about everyday Polynesian mores for that subject to need detailing or even summary here. But there are a few remarkable aspects unique to Raiatea or at least stemming from that island, which illustrate its individuality and its imaginative creativity, its role as the wellspring, as I see it, of Polynesian culture as a whole and not merely its role of "grand emporium of idolatry."

Teuira Henry writes in her *Ancient Tahiti*:

"Havai'i (Invoked-space-that-filled) was of undisputed prestige among the islands in ancient times and is still the proudest island in all the Society group, being the center of their history, their religion, and their heraldry. Formerly as is shown in pure archaic records by its ancient bards, which are corroborated by its sister island groups, Havai'i exercised a political and moral sway as the emporium of all the Maori tribes of Polynesia.

"Dividing Havai'i equally in two by a meridian, all the islands on the eastern side were named Te-ao-uri (Dark-land), those on the west Te-ao-tea (Light-land); these names were shortened into Uri (Dark), for east Havai'i, and Tea (Light), for west Havai'i; and in the course of time they were blended together, and Uri-e-tea (Dark and Light) became a new name for the whole island which

* The *upa upa* is of course the original of the better known to us, *hula hula.*

Opposite
This photograph of the great "coronation" stone, whose full name is Te-papa-tea-ia-orea (the white slab of investiture) was taken in 1929. Posing beside it (for scale) are two generations of the most eminent anthropologists of Polynesia: Sir Peter Buck, who later became director of the Bishop Museum and author, after many monumental scholarly works, of *Vikings of the Sunrise*; and Dr. Kenneth P. Emory, who is at present generally recognized as the Dean of Polynesian anthropology and archaeology.

The sweet potato, the *'umara* in Raiatea and the central Polynesian islands, *kumara* in most of the other groups, originated in South America and yet was found throughout Polynesia when the white man arrived. How did it get there? Dr. Buck was convinced that the Polynesians sailed to Peru (or thereabouts) and brought it back. This most cherished of vegetables is proof positive for many experts of deliberate, long-distance, two-way voyaging. Others are skeptical. I am not.

was gradually corrupted by some into Iore-tea (White-rat). The name Ra'iatea (clear-sky) was of last adoption and the following is its history.

"Not long after the Flood and after royal families from Opoa had established themselves in Tahiti, there was a high chief of Papara, named Atea, who was the proprietor of the marae named Maha'i-atea (Expansive-mitigation). He went to Uri-e-tea, where he married a princess of Opoa named Ra'i (Sky).

"The wife became pregnant and meanwhile the husband, being a valiant warrior, was called off by some of his clans to battle; so in taking leave of his wife he said pathetically:

Ia fanau ra to taua tamarii e, eiaha e faarue ia'u i te i'oa i nia iho. Mai te mea ra e e potii, e topa ia oe ia Rai nui-atea; e tamaiti ra, o Atea noa ae ia.	When our child is born, do not exclude me from naming it. If it be a daughter, name her Rai-nui-atea (Great-expansive-sky); and should it be a son, let the name be simply Atea.

"To this the wife agreed, and the child that came, being a girl, was named Rai-nui-atea, after her mother and father conjointly.

"Chief Atea was slain in battle, and he was deeply mourned by the bereaved princess and all the royal family of Opoa, so that eventually the name was transmitted from the child to the land, when it was contracted into Rai-atea (Expansive-sky)."

Opoa

First let us consider Opoa and its environs. Opoa on the east coast, about 13 kilometers by lagoon south of the present "capital" of Uturoa, was the most sacred area of the whole sacred island. Above it towered the highest mountains, the dwelling places of the gods. It must be remembered that the gods did not live in heaven or the sky, as in most other religions. They lived above, but definitely neighborly to their mortal descendants: each could keep an eye on the other. The parallel to Mount Olympus is obvious.

The mana of Opoa extended up the broad valley that reaches from its bay, up into the mountains. Mana is not an easy word to translate, but it was of paramount importance to the old-time Polynesian and it still has a very palpable consequence.It denotes power and virtue, a mystical force possessed in various degrees by both gods and men. It is palpable in that it can be passed from one person to another. It can be acquired peacefully, as Tafai

Ru, the god who raised the sky from the earth, circumnavigated the world with his sister Hina, who was the pilot of their canoe. When they had sailed around (probably around the horizon), they sought a final landing place and, rejecting all the other islands, Ru sang to Hina:

"I am drawing, drawing to land
Teapori, O Teapori*
I am drawing to land,
Now hold steadily on to Havai'i"
Then cried his sister, Hina,
"Upon the foaming waves
O Ru! land is looming up.
What land is it?"
"It is Havai'i; let its watchword
be Havai'i that towers
exceeding in glory,
Great Havai'i when enraged
in its beauty."

There they settled, but Hina's love of discovery did not cease. One evening when the full moon was shining invitingly, she set off in her canoe to make it a visit. On arriving, she was so pleased with the moon that she stepped into it, leaving to the mercy of the sea her canoe, which was never seen again. Thus she became goddess of the moon. The shadows of the moon were believed to be an ora tree (banyan) and from its numerous branches Hina made bark cloth for the gods. One day she broke off a branch, stamping petulently with such force that it flew out into space and ultimately arrived at Opoa in Raiatea, where it struck root and was the first tree of its kind ever seen in the world.

*The name of his canoe.

Opposite
The first record we have of the marae Taputapuatea is this original wash drawing by Parkinson. He does not name it specifically, but I think we can be almost certain because it is obviously a leeward island marae, which is quite distinct from the windward or Tahitian type

shown here. Cook, when Parkinson was with him on his first voyage, stopped first at Opoa, and Taputapuatea was the obvious and most evident marae. Moreover, the scale as denoted by the ladies in the foreground; the hog, which is probably the one described by Banks on page 139; the presence of the large tamanu tree; and especially, in the background, the repetition of the double canoe shed whose separate drawing on page 130 is labeled "View in Ulietea;" all convince me that this is our first view of what might be called the "source" marae, the St Peter's, of all central Polynesia. The decorative stakes were characteristic of all maraes, though their function is obscure.

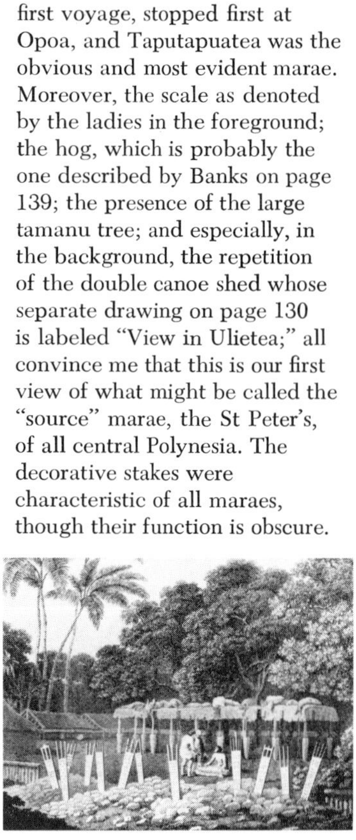

received it by opening his mouth over the top of his mother's head. Mana resides in the head, and its presence there is the reason why no one should ever pat a Polynesian on his head. Indeed, if a chief was seated, his companions or household would drop to their knees before, behind, or beside him, when passing. Nor would you allow your shadow in the sunset to ride over a chief's head, even at a long distance. But mana is not exclusive to chiefs. It can reside in the master of the household or in any good man or woman. It was of prime importance to a taua, a priest of the temple, a canoe builder, especially to a navigator, a house-builder, a guardian or protector of fishermen, a weather prophet, and so on and on. It was also of the greatest import to a warrior, the main power by which he could defeat his enemy. And in the defeat of a foe, mana could pass, as a result of violence, to the victor from the slain. When a man died, his skull retained mana and was kept in the eaves of the house, imparting benevolence to the whole household. Even the bones of a lucky fisherman were stolen, if his relatives were not wary, to make fishhooks with special mystique. And, of course, mana could pass from a sacrificial victim to his host by eating his flesh.

So Opoa was the seat of the mana of Raiatea, and it centered most concentratedly in the great marae of Taputapuatea, which lies on the flat point extending from Opoa out into the lagoon. I write of Opoa as though it were a village or cluster of habitations. It is today, but before the missionaries came and gathered their disciples close about their church, the people of the district of Opoa (as in all other districts in the pre-contact ocean islands) were scattered at comfortable intervals along the shores and up the valleys. In many island groups where valleys or districts were wont to go to war with each other, forts were built, usually on hilltops or even mountaintops, and concentration of the population was intense in times of strife. But neither Raiatea nor any of the other islands of the Society group built forts. There was inter-island strife, especially with the Poraporans, who were notorious raiders, but only rarely intra-island warfare until Cook came and supplied muskets to the power-hungry Pomares on Tahiti.

Taputapuatea, according to Miss Henry, means "Sacrifices from abroad," and it was the original marae, and much the largest in the whole group. It was not always so called and was not always an international marae. At a very remote period, before the god Oro was born at Opoa, it was the national marae of Havaiki and was called Tinirauhinimatatepapa o Feoro, which means "Fruitful myriads who engraved the rocks of Feoro" (usually shortened to Feoro).* When Oro was born, Taaroa, his father, gave him Opoa and its marae as a place to live. He soon became very powerful, and the people of all the lands beyond the shores of Havaiki acknowledged him as the supreme everyday god of the earth and sky. The name Feoro was changed to Vaiotaha, meaning "Water of the man o' war bird," because the man o'war bird was Oro's shadow and the water meant human blood. To his marae were taken most of the heads of decapitated warriors. The skulls were cleaned and stacked in shining white rows in the crevices and nooks of the black stones of the temple.

* A very recent archaeological discovery may possibly be a verification of this ancient legendary history. When Yosi Sinoto of the Bishop Museum was restoring the ahu of Taputapuatea in 1971 he discovered a much older, smaller ahu inside of, and encompassed by, the large one that has dominated the famous temple from Cook's day to our own.

Over
The two splendid photographs by Axel Poignant on page 108 show Taputapuatea as it is today, recently restored by Dr. Yosi Sinoto, head of the Anthropology Department at the Bishop Museum. The top picture is the front of the *ahu* or altar, with its small square "podium" where the priests probably stood when conducting ceremonies and making offerings. The upright stones are the usual "backrests" or "reserved seats" for the highest chiefs.

The lower photograph is the back or sea side of the ahu. This marae structure is by far the longest (though not the highest) of any marae in the islands.

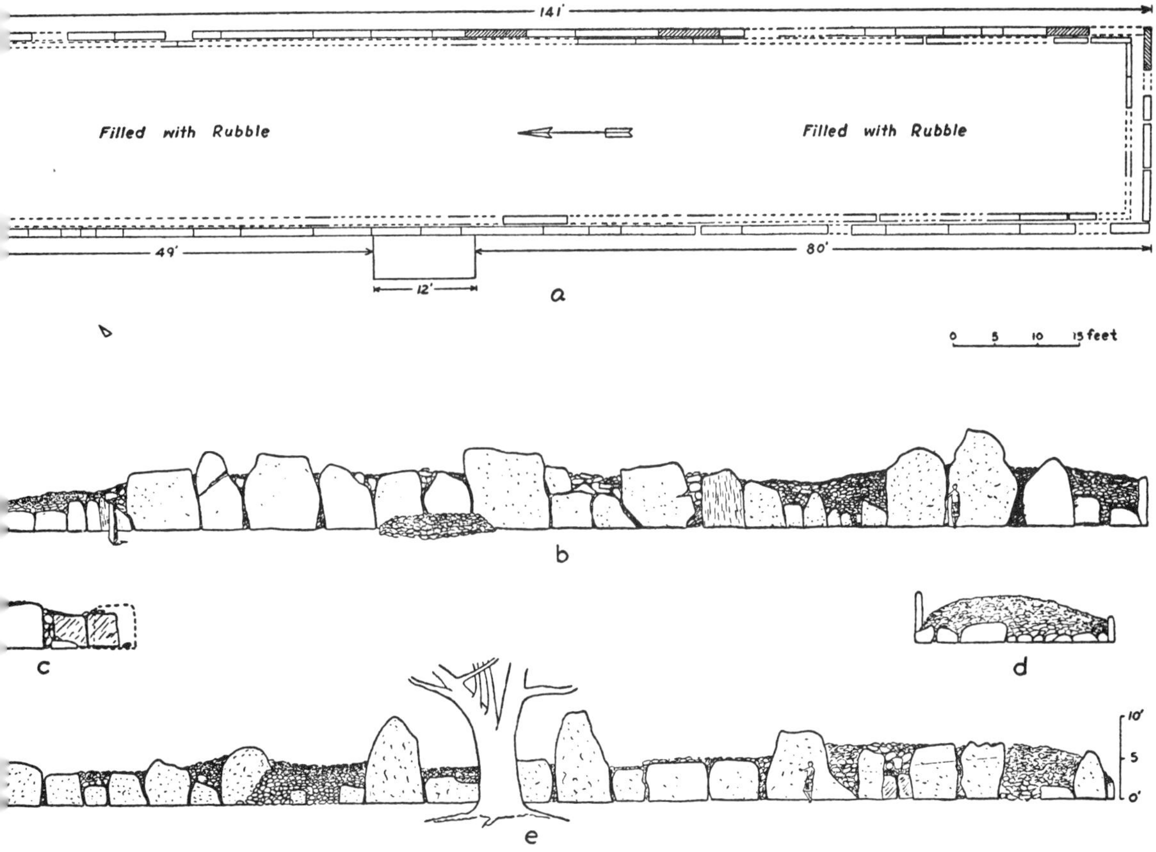

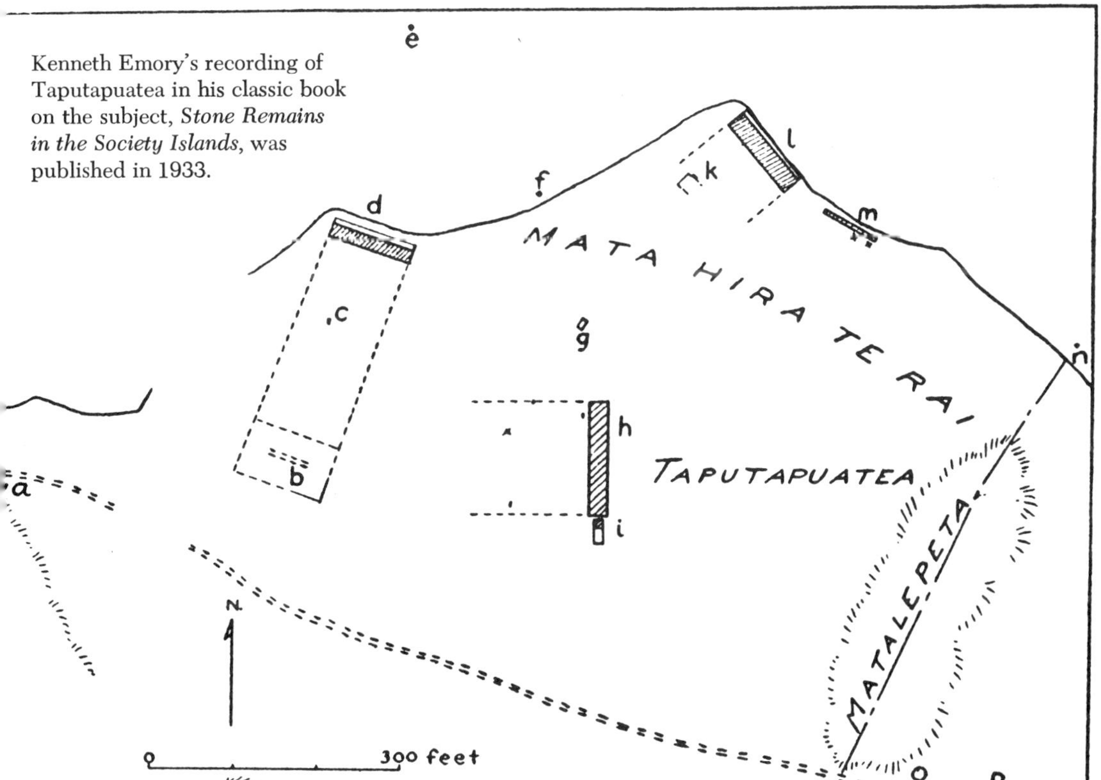

Kenneth Emory's recording of Taputapuatea in his classic book on the subject, *Stone Remains in the Society Islands,* was published in 1933.

It should be noted that although I have called Taputapuatea the "source" marae from which all others were apparently derived, it was not the first marae in Opoa. This was Vaearae on the river, about a half mile up the valley where Taaroa "broke through the sky" and first put his foot upon the earth. *Vaearae* means Foot-of-heaven.

Bleached with age, says Miss Henry, these lay untouched for generations, until tourists began to collect them. Those left were quickly hidden by the natives. All other marae were founded by bringing a sacred stone from Taputapuatea or one of its descendant maraes. It was there that chiefs were brought for investiture, from the Cook islands, Rarotonga, Aitutaki, Mangaia, six hundred miles to the southwest. Some say they were even brought all the way up from Aotearoa (the original name for New Zealand), some 2000 miles from Raiatea. For that reason this marae has been called the international temple of Polynesia, though that seems to be a foreigner's not a native's designation.

The ceremonies held at Taputapuatea were much the same as those held on other marae throughout Polynesia. Indeed, the others probably derived their pattern from the great temple of the homeland. There were the celebrations of the rites of passage: birth, circumcision, puberty, marriage, death. For these, especially birth and death, marvelous ceremonial objects of art were created: ceremonial paddles and canoe models for the child who was to be a great sailor, adzes so elaborate they could never be used for the canoe builder and house builder, fanciful hooks for the fisherman, and fanciful spears for the warrior. More important artistically were the beautifully carved tikis, the receptacle statues of gods, when the help of one or another of these gods or of his mana was desired on important social occasions, such as war or drought or famine or the setting forth on a great voyage or the welcoming of an important chiefly party from overseas (always such a chief would approach Raiatea through the pass that led to Opoa and would first touch land at Taputapuatea). Other ceremonials of import were auguries and prophecies, human sacrifice to appease an angry god or to give conclusive authority to any project or occasion of outstanding communal significance.

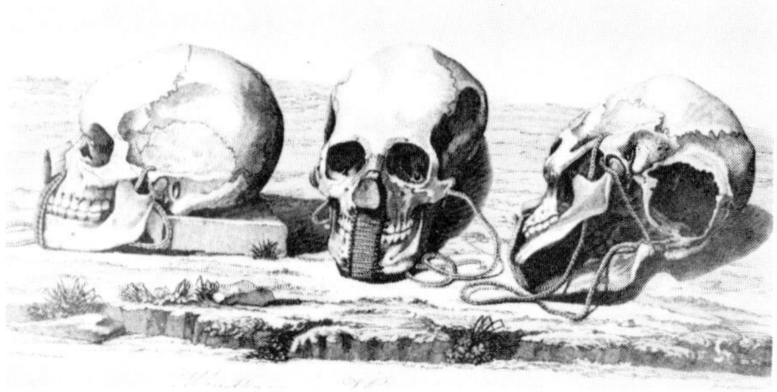

Here, too, in the grounds of the temple stood and still stands the great "coronation" stone, Tepapaoruea, "the rock of investment," where the heirs to paramount chiefhood received their ultimate authority. This stone stands about eight feet high today, but in old pictures it seems closer to nine feet. It was said that the great ancient Tamatoas were as tall as this stone, which must be an exaggeration, but one of the early missionaries measured the Tamatoa then current and found him to be "6 feet 11½ inches and powerfully and beautifully proportioned."

Also upon this widespread flat point of land were, and are still, the imposing big family marae of the Tamatoa, as well as another smaller marae (probably for canoe landings and other more mundane purposes), a large stone dance platform, and foundations of houses for priests and for special occasions. It was in short a busy, multipurpose, and awesome area. Women were not allowed, not even to watch the goings-on, except perhaps in the case of a high chiefess. (Amongst the arii or very highborn, women ranked equally with men in many Polynesian societies, and this was unquestionably so in Raiatea where, if a female was the closest of kin to a deceased chief, she would inherit the supreme power and pass it on to her offspring. But males first, of course.)

This leads us to another exclusively Raiatean feature, the Tamatoa. They were highest of the high of all the chiefly families of the central island groups. Only they could wear the red girdle made of parakeet feathers, brought first from the forests of Raiatea, but later, when the parakeets there had been destroyed, from Rarotonga. When a new "king" or "queen" was inaugurated it was a time of great moment to all the islanders. Extensive preparation of food and dress were made for several months, but the greatest work of all was the preparation of a new section of the red girdle. This was a network of finely woven flax, over a background of banyan cloth. The stem of a red feather was set in each little hole and caught in a lockstitch by a long polished needle of human bone. The sacred needle was never taken out of the work which was intended to last forever, a new lappet being added for each reign. A human victim was sacrificed for the three stages, each with its own traditional name: "piercing the cloth," "putting in the needle," and "completing the maro." During these rites, the gods sent flashes of lightning and peals of thunder, even when the sky was cloudless.

The royal red maro of the Tamatoa was the longest of all—being twenty-one feet long and six inches wide when, upon his conversion, the last Tamatoa to wear it gave it to the missionaries. They in turn sent it to their museum in

The Tamatoa family marae on the water's edge is a handsome structure. This too has been recently restored. Altogether the whole area might now be called the "cathedral close" of the Pacific, the most impressive religious monument of central Polynesia. In its restoration, except for the numerous skulls, it now appears much as it was originally, the primary active religious center before the white man came.

London, but when their collection was later turned over to the British Museum, in about 1920, the famous girdle was missing and has not been found since. (One hopes that one of the brethren was light-fingered and that it may turn up some day in the attic of one of his descendants.) The high chiefs of Tahiti, even though richer in lands and more powerful in warriors, were restricted to the yellow girdle, from the feathers of the golden plover, always acknowledged as secondary to the maro ura. Naturally, Tamatoa sisters and daughters, younger brothers and younger sons, could and did, intermarry with the chiefs and chiefesses of other islands, but only the single ruling Tamatoa of Raiatea could ever wear the sacred red girdle.

Fire Walking

Probably the most dramatic spectacle to originate* in the island was the fire walking, although perhaps its consequence was more striking to outsiders (and more recently to missionaries, visitors, and tourists) than to the native islanders. This has been too well publicized to warrant description here. We need only note that it originated in Raiatea.

* There seems little doubt that, for these central Pacific island groups, fire walking originated in Raiatea. It is now the only island where the ceremony is still performed. But it is also well-known in Fiji, and that may be its ultimate ancestry.

This illustration is by Paul Huguenin, who was director of education in the Leeward Islands before the turn of the century. An artist as well as an educator and writer, his lovely book *Raiatea La Sacrée* was published in 1902.

Miss Henry tell us, "The breadfruit was born on Raiatea and in ancient times it was always called uru (head) until long, long ago a king of Raiatea, named Mahoru took that name, and it was then called maiore: but gradually the name maiore wore out and *uru* again became the common name of the fruit."

This is typical of central Polynesia and an illustration of the people's respect for the whims of the high born, as well as their propensity for name changing, as fickle as that of Paris for new styles. Whenever a chief or chiefess took unto himself or herself a new name, that word became tapu and, no matter how common coin, was apparently readily changed, perhaps even gladly, for monotony was a fact of life. They were inventive people with quick minds who had nothing to invent, so they played word games and thus enriched and refreshed their language, retaining always in their memories the antecedents of these impulsive irrational switches. It is particularly interesting here as an illustration of the power of a Raiatean "king." Breadfruit was as basic to Polynesian life as bread is to ours, so such a radical change would affect everyone in the islands. And it must have done so, because today breadfruit is always called maiore in the Marquesas, 500 miles from Raiatea, and it is still often used in the other islands as an alternate to uru.

Another much more widely known example of name changing is the decision of one of the high Tahitian chiefs, Tu, to change his name to Pomare because he coughed in the cold one night in the woods. "Po" means night and "mare" cough. Although he was not actually the highest chief of the island, Pomare was the most ambitious of his time, and he persuaded Captain Cook to back him with fire arms and, thus, in European eyes, to "crown" him. We might say that in effect it was Cook's gullibility that founded the Pomare "dynasty"—and dealt one of the most degenerating blows to Tahitian culture.

Opposite
Again we can find no finer illustrator than Sydney Parkinson. This is his painting of *uru* or breadfruit, which has been appreciated many times in the text.

Opposite
Gauguin's title for this painting, one of his masterpieces, is *Te aa no Ariois*, which has been translated by its owner, Mr. William Paley, "Queen of the Ariois." Actually the title means the "root" of the Arioi. The Arioi society never had a "queen" or even a paramount chiefess, but this is Gauguin's imaginative portrait of Vairaumati, the lovely maiden of Pora Pora who, impregnated by Oro the great god of Opoa and at the time the most powerful of all Taaroa's sons, conceived the founders of the Arioi society. Their seductive disciples were triumphing over all other Polynesian cults until the scandalized missionaries declared the society their foremost enemy and quashed it completely.

Gauguin was fascinated, perhaps obsessed, with the Arioi, as we shall see again presently. The society might be said to epitomize his love affair with the Polynesians. This is his second painting of Vairaumati. The first, now in the Hermitage in Leningrad, did not satisfy him. For both, the model was Teha'amana, his thirteen-year-old vahine at the time.

Another facet of the old-time culture stemming from our little island, and specifically from Opoa, deserves special and more lengthy attention. That is the Arioi society. I wish I could set down the particulars which I think it deserves, but they are exasperatingly nebulous, hidden in the cloud of prudishness in which they were obscured not only by missionaries, who sought so diligently to eliminate every trace of these obscene, evil entertainers, but even by the earlier explorers, whose observations were usually published by responsible gentlemen whose morals were almost as shocked as those of the ordained brethren. I, in turn, was almost as shocked as they to discover that there is only one reference to Arioi in the Index to the famous *Journal of the Polynesian Society*, the grand emporium, since 1892, of scholarly studies of Polynesia. The reference is to a review of a monograph by Mühlmann in a widely-known German periodical. I find him as disappointingly unspecific as the others. He says that the best description is John Forster's; the nub of it reads:

"As long as the chiefs of these islanders were few, the rest of the nation, preserved a kind of respect for these leaders, who then it seems, were the heroes and best warriors of the nation. But opulence, the fertility of soil and climate, and idleness at last increased the race of chiefs to such a degree, that the wise men of the nation, the great chiefs of the provinces and the whole nation itself, could not but be alarmed at their too great number, and the disturbances which were doubtless too often made by an idle, athletic, and numerous set of men. The respect which the rest of the nation still had for their chiefs, and the great bodily strength of these drones, whose force was unimpaired by labour, and daily inflamed by a preternatural indulgence in the choicest fruit, and the fat of the land, made it more and more difficult to quell the riots of these turbulent men. The married women have in all these isles a great respect shewn to them, and their influence is great in all public and private affairs; and as soon as the heir of a family is born, the father in a certain manner loses his importance. These two circumstances made

Most commentators, indeed all that I have found, say that she is holding a sprouting coconut in her hand. But this seems to me impossible. Gauguin was not a one to be meticulous about literal sizes and proportions, but a sprouting coconut would still have its husk on and be as big as a football. Note that the mangoes are normal. Moreover the coconut sprout has a distinct stem as you can see in Jacques Boullaire's accurate drawing on page 111. More likely, I think, she is holding the sprouting seed of the hutu reva, the sacred marae tree.

young men of rank and property averse to marriage; and as they felt the strong calls of nature under the influence of a powerful sun, they endeavoured to gratify their sensuality in such a manner as was easy and most obvious; and as the other sex was excited by the same causes to indulge themselves in sensual pleasure, the consequence was natural, that every kind of debauchery was introduced. These scenes of lewdness nevertheless, could not be at first very common; but the children who were born in consequence of this practice, became the object of serious public consideration; they had not been born in regular marriage, nor was it always possible to point out the true father; they were therefore deprived of the right of inheritance, on account of the uncertainty of their offspring; but continued to be stiled *Arees*, and were allowed to belong to the family of chiefs, already grown too numerous, turbulent, and powerful. As these chiefs, according to a former observation, were the best warriors of the nations, the great chiefs and sage men thought it prudent to institute an order of men, who should have great perogatives, and great honours paid to them, and who were to be the chief warriors; and that they might not be too much attached to their wives and children, they were forbid marriage; and in the beginning of the institution, they were directed to abstain from all kinds of venery, as a practice that checked the boldness of spirit, and deprived men of that bodily strength so much required in their warriors. This society is called *Arreeoy*, and it still subsisting; though somewhat altered from its primitive institution. There is no prerogative which a man likes more to boast of at the Society-islands, than that of an *Arreeoy*, they all belong to the class of warriors: as soon as an *Arreeoy* from another country appears, he is kindly received by the first *Arreeoy*, whom he meets; they exchange presents in cloth and garments, and he is entertained by his new host, with all the demonstration of friendship, and with the most unbounded hospitality. At certain stated times of the year the *Arreeoys* of one island remove to another and there the days are spent in great feasts, wherein a profusion of the dainties of the country are consumed, and the nights are spent in music and

dances, which are said to be remarkably lascivious, and likewise in the embraces of some girls, who officiate on these occasions like the priestesses and nymphs of the Paphian and Amathusian Goddess among the Greeks. We saw about seventy canoes sailing in one day from Huaheine to Raietea, with more than seven hundred people of both sexes on board, in order to assist at one of these feasts; when we arrived at Raietea, we found these *Arreeoys* removed from the Eastern side of the island where they first had landed to its Western shore, and there we saw every house and shed crowded with people, and in every large house, we observed heaps of provisions piled up, which were preparing by their women; and fishes, fowls, hogs, and dogs, were likewise dressed on this solemn occasion. During the night we could see these houses illuminated, and frequently heard the sound of their drums, which are used at their dramatic dances. And

These dancing girls painted by James Webber, who was official artist on the third voyage, may or may not have been Arioi. Certainly they are very properly dressed (or overdressed), but the Arioi were versatile entertainers and not all of their dances were "lascivious." At any rate this is the best graphic dance recording that we have from early contact.

in a few days afterwards they removed to *O-Taha.* and we were told, that they would even go as far as *Bora-Bora* before they would think of returning. So that several weeks must be spent in these feasts of *Arreeoys.* It is impossible that the frequent cohabitation with women, should not now and then be productive of an offspring; nay some of the modern *Arreeoys*, are so far degenerated, that they regularly keep a mistress, which, to all intents and purposes, is similar to a temporary wife, such as Muhammedans are used to marry for a certain time only. But as this custom was contrary to the spirit of the original institution of *Arreeoys* the Sages of the nation made another law, according to which, all infants, the offspring of the connexion of the Arreeoys with women, should be instantly killed after their birth, because the increase of the Arees was thought to be detrimental to the state, and the original engagements of the *Arreeoys*, never to cohabit with women, would else have been entirely defeated. *Boba*, the chief of O-Taha, was an Arreeoy, and nevertheless kept *Teinamai*, as a mistress, who was with child by him, at our second return to the Society-islands, and told us the child would be stifled the moment it was brought forth. Regulation and custom have established

This dancing scene from Hawkesworth was concocted in London, based fancifully on sketches by Cook's artists, and though it is more voluptuous it is obviously far from accurate. Here is a Greek temple with coconut columns, a Ganymede in the corner, and a Pan playing a nose flute. But then Hawkesworth was a popularizer and his large, handsomely engraved and lavishly illustrated three-volume account of four famous voyages was widely popular in London at the time.

this inhuman practice; and nations which are not yet acquainted with those refined and sublime principles of virtue, which are established by the introduction of christianity into Europe, have frequently sacrificed the observation of a moral or social virtue to the greater security of the state, and even to a device for preventing imaginary evils; nay, which is worse, to a method of promoting either a martial spirit, or for teaching the stratagems of war. Thus for instance, the Spartans now and then sent their youths out upon the business of killing Helotes; or ordered them to steal. However, we found these inhuman practices to be the effects of OPULENCE, LUXURY and SENSUALITY in a nation, which upon the whole, is not destitute of humanity, but rather inclined to practice kindness and good-nature, in a manner which would do honour to a more enlightened and civilized race of men."

Other comments by other early observers seem to be more pointed and particular than Forster's mighty moralizing:

Captain Cook: "A young man, nearly six feet high, performed the rites of Venus with a little girl about eleven or twelve years of age, before several of our people, and a great number of the natives, without the least sense of its being indecent or improper, but, as appeared, in perfect conformity to the custom of the place. Among the spectators were several women of superior rank, who may properly be said to have assisted at the ceremony; for they gave instructions to the girl how to perform her part, which, young as she was, she did not seem much to stand in need of."

James Morrison: "If an Areeuoy preserves any of His Children (which they seldom do till they advance in Years and the Fire of their Youthful Passions is a little quench'd) they are not then treated with so much respect as when Batchelors & are then denominated Areeuoy fwhanownow or a childbearing Areeuoy and are not entertained at the feasts till after the Batchelors are served tho they are always looked on as part of the Society and treated as such."

Over
Poetua, a specific dancing girl of the Arioi, whose portrait by Webber appears on page 123 following, was a daughter of Orea, high chief of Raiatea and a charmer by all accounts. She was even praised by the missionaries and yet obviously envied by them, perhaps symbolizing their competition with the Arioi, where she was evidently a star performer. She

The Arioi were an exclusive, mysterious society devoted to the god of war, Oro. They are reported to have been very ancient, but their devotion to Oro must have been fairly recent when our Europeans first recoiled from their performances. Oro had only recently supplanted Tane as the chief god of Opoa; probably no more than fifty years, or a couple of generations, before Cook. The cult of Oro spread rapidly, however, and the Arioi were its most effective disciples. Though Oro was the god of war, the Arioi were apparently not warlike according to most reports and differing from Forster. In the main they seem to have been entertainers (and, according to Danielsson, highly attractive proselitizers of their sexy faith), who travelled as a troupe about their island and annually made extended tours to the other islands. In many places on other islands local branches of the society built huge houses for the entertainments, sometimes as much as 800 feet long. The revels were usually held at night, lit with strings of candlenuts and large bonfires, and were such rousing occasions that it was said even the crickets sang with joy.

In times of war the Arioi were exempt from all threat or danger and could even entertain unmolested on the battlefield. They colored their bodies with the yellowish-orange dye of the tumeric, blackened their faces, and probably for the most part sang and danced in the nude. Their theatricals were mainly pantomime, and they were allowed, even encouraged, to satirize local chiefs, especially pompous ones, in a fashion that resembled perhaps the function of the privileged jester in our medieval courts.

"When a would-be entrant at last was ready he wore a girdle of yellow plaintain or *ti* leaves round his loins, his face was stained with *mat*, or scarlet dye; his brow decorated with a shade of curiously plaited yellow cocoa-nut leaves, his hair perfumed with powerfully scented oil, and ornamented with a profusion of fragrant flowers. Thus arrayed, disfigured, and adorned, he rushed through the crowd assembled round the house in which the actors or dancers were performing, and, leaping into the circle, joined with seeming frantic wildness in the dance or pantomime."

—William Ellis

seems to be noted in everyone's diary. Think of yourself or conceive of yourself as a member of that magical voyage! Here is a sampling.

Cook: "The chief enterain'd us with a Comedy or Dramatic Heava [dance] . . . the Musick consisted of three drums, the actors were Seven Men and one Woman, the chief's daughter . . . at whose Shrine many pretty things were offered by her numerous Votarists and I believe was one great inducement why her father gave us these entertainments."

Pickersgill, the Master's mate, was particularly smitten and was invited into her room "to watch her dress."

Wales: "She was in truth a cute Girl and deficient in no one point, that I know of, unless it was Chastity, and as to that it was not seemingly considered as one of the Cardinal Virtues at our house."

George Forster: "We had alrady fat fome time admift the principal ladies of the ifland, when the actreffes appeared. One of them was Poyadua, the fair daughter of the chief Orea. . . . They moved to the found of the drums, and . . . a fong. Their attitudes and geftures were much varied, and fometimes might admit of being conftrued into wantonefs; but they were entirely free from that pofitive degree of grofs indesency which the chafte eyes of English ladies of fafhion are *forced* to behold at the opera."

On the third voyage Poetua, with her husband and brother, was taken prisoner by Cook, kidnapped, one might say, and held as ransom for the return of three deserters. "The Raiateans reasoning that two could play at the game of hostages, plotted the seizure of Cook and Clerke on shore at their daily bath. One almost regrets that the plot broke down," concludes Dr. Beaglehole wistfully.

Gauguin illustrated the origin o the Arioi in one of his notebook Here is a retelling of it partly from Teiura Henry and partly from Paul Gauguin.

Oro and his wife dwelt with many gods in the firmament where he reigned as god of peace, the emblem of which was a triangle of three spears laid together in opposition or impotence, ∇.

One day he pushed his wife down to the earth where she became a great heap of sand and remained so ever after. Wh Oro became lonely without a wife, his two sisters descended to the earth to find him a new one. They searched everywhere in Tahiti, Huahine, Tahaa, and even in Raiatea, his native birthplace, but the women were all too coarse and common. At last they found a royal maiden of surpassing beauty in Pora Pora named Vairaumati. "Enchanted were they with her beauty! Her face was as the noontide light, and the luster of

dark eyes shone forth like
: from the deep-blue sky.
kindly welcomed them, and
greeted her with flashes
ghtning which made her
ne, like themselves, and she
e them be seated with her
er mat. 'A great errand has
ight you to me, O great
desses?'
'es, we have indeed a great
nd! We have come to ask you
ecome the wife of our
her, Oro, god of firmament.'
s he handsome?' enquired the

'es! He is handsomer than
he sons of men and is ever
thful,' they replied. So it was
nged that this lovely maid
to become the spouse of the
t god Oro."
)ro was highly pleased and
y next morning he came down
arth clothed in a cloud on a
liant rainbow. Soon after,
marriage took place, with the
e providing many valuable
. Oro, who had no terrestrial
ents, was embarrassed, and to save himself from ridicule he returned to the sky and transformed his two brothers into two fine hogs, a boar and a sow, who were never to be killed. He led them down by the rainbow and presented them to his wife with a cachet of red feathers. These two pigs then became gods of the Arioi Society (yet to be organized). The following night, the sow produced five fine little male pigs. The first was the sacred pig of the Arioi; the second was sent to sea and became a porpoise; the third was a pet for Oro's wife, the fourth was "for sending to different lands," and the fifth was sacred to the marae, "marked with a ring of sacred sennit through its nose."

Vairaumati became pregnant and her son was King Tamatoa, the first Arioi on this earth. Oro at length decided he must leave and he ascended to the heavens in a great column of fire, leaving all the people of the earth gasping with astonishment.

The Arioi revels, by all reports from white men, were extravagently licentious, obscene, and unspeakable. Just what that means is difficult to ascertain specifically. The society was long since disbanded, and even forgotten, before our present age of frank expression on such matters had even been dreamed of. From hints and vague allusions one can be fairly certain that sexual intercourse was not only performed in public, but probably openly flaunted in an exciting variety of aspects and sensuality. Yet their's must have been much more than pornographic burlesque. When they sailed in, in their great double canoes, sometimes in fleets of 70 or 80 vessels, they were rousingly welcomed everywhere, feasted and celebrated, by the high chiefs, as well as the populace at large. They exhausted whole neighborhoods of their foodstuffs and their energies, but, when they left, their hosts sighed with content and wondered how they could get themselves through the boredom of the ensuing year, to the next grand carousel.

The Arioi society was tightly organized and its rules strict, so strict that if a member broke them he or she was dismissed in disgrace and became to all a permanent outcast. There were eight levels or ranks in the society, each marked by its special clothing and special tatu. It took many years and painstaking training to reach the top: only a very few ever attained it, and they came from the highest chiefly families. Sexual morals were entirely free —or we might say absent. They associated with each other in a gay, communal fashion though one can be fairly certain that there was no homosexuality. They practised rigid abortion or infanticide. Evidently a member could resign, but if she or he returned to ordinary life they would have been disgraced and have been punished by ostracism.

Captain William Bligh, in his typically pithy way, handed down a few judgements on the "Erreeoys": "Celebacy without blemish proves the source of constant transgression . . . and the Society . . . has become disgraceful to human Nature, altho it may be said to have been founded in wisdom."

"It appears however that the Erreeoys from leading an

Idle and gay life have among them the finest Women of the Island. They are always in large Parties. Always drest with the greatest profusion of the best Cloth and are generally fat and Saucy."

"The women have too great an intercourse with different men . . . I have known a Man to have done the Act in the presence of his own Wife and it is a common thing for the Wife to assist the Husband in these Amours."

The society was highly skilled in theatrical arts and greatly respected. Of the mysterious power which held them together very little is known or has been reported, and why and how they spread the gospel of Oro I cannot fathom from the records. But the fact is that they did spread their gospel most effectively, because all the old conventional gods of the islands were melting away before this angry and bloody, yet paradoxically enticing and kindly, newcomer. Perhaps this is one reason the people took so readily to Christianity when the missionaries arrived.

THE FAMOUS FLEET

To this telling over of the "wonders" unique to Raiatea, a few more might be added. First, it should be cited that there exists a strong probability that New Zealand was settled, as Beaglehole says, by "the emigration of 'The Fleet' from Raiatea, which gave New Zealand its Maori population circa 1350 A.D." (This of course was by far the largest offspring of our little island, having a population of perhaps 400,000 before the white man came.)

Another unusual product of the island was a native named Tupaia. Joseph Banks writes of Tupaia, (with footnotes by Beaglehole):

"This morn Tupia came on board, renewd his resolves of going with us to England, a circumstance which gives me much satisfation. He is certainly a most proper man, well born, chief *Tahowa** or priest of this Island consequently skilld in the mysteries of their religion; but what makes him more than any thing else desireable is his experience in the navigation of these people and knowledge of the Islands in these seas; he has told us the names of above 70, the most of which he has himself been at.† The captn refuses to take him on his own account, in my opinion sensibly enough, the government will never in all human probability take any notice of him; I therefore have resolvd to take him. Thank heaven I have a sufficiency and I do not know why I may not keep him as a curiosity, as well as some of my neighbours do lions and tygers at a larger expence than he will probably ever put me to; the amusement I shall have in his future conversation and the benefit he will be of to this ship, as well as what he may be if another should be sent into these seas, will I think fully repay me."

Tupaia proved much more valuable to Cook than any number of lions and tygers. He directed him to many unknown islands. At all of them he could converse with the natives in a sort of pan-Polynesian language that he was the first, in the white man's knowledge, to demonstrate. He was a highly skilled navigator who, through all the

* *Tahua* (cf. Maori *tohunga*, and other Polynesian variants).

† This is rather an overstatement. Cook, in the list of islands which he gives from Tupaia's information, marks no more than twelve that Tupaia said he had himself visited, and one of those was Raiatea, his native place. Cook writes, "This man had been with us the most part of the time we had been upon the Island which gave us an oppertunity to know some thing of him: we found him to be a very intelligent person and to know more of the Geography of the Islands situated in these seas, their produce and the religion laws and customs of the inhabitants then any one we had met with and was the likeliest person to answer our purpose; for these reasons and at the request of Mr. Banks I received him on board together with a young boy his servant." Tupaia came of a family well-known for its skill in navigation.

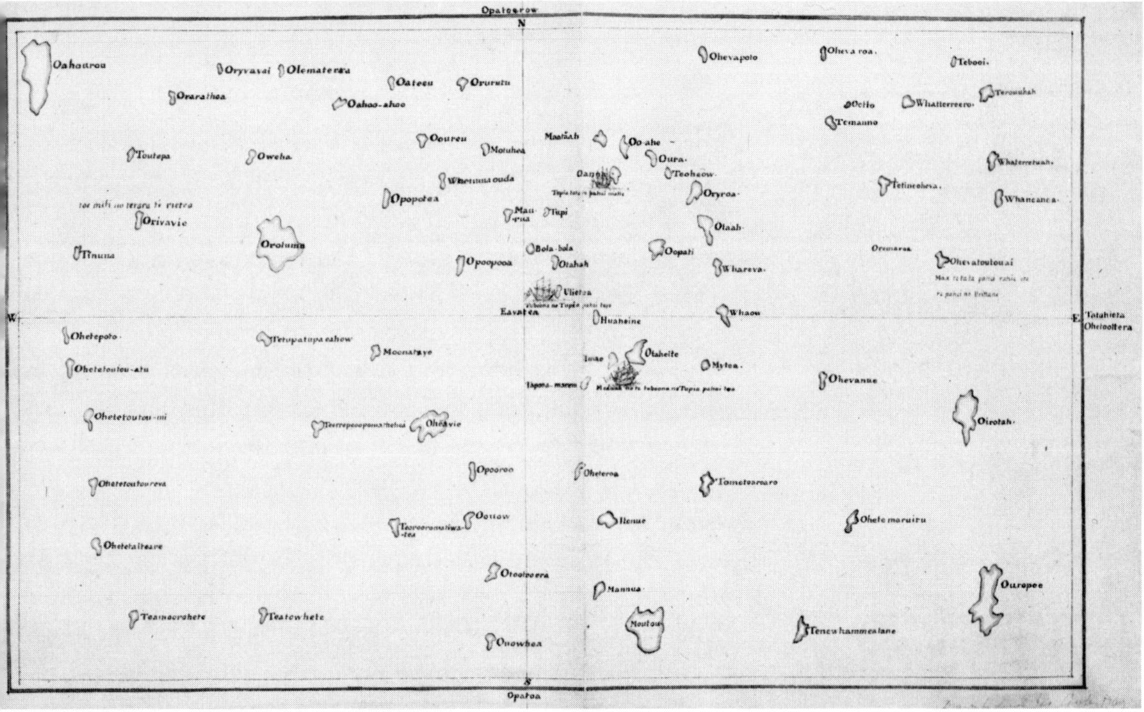

Endeavour's wanderings from Raiatea to Batavia, where he died of the local plague of malaria, could always point correctly to where, as Cook knew by his compass, the island of Tahiti lay. This was a voyage lasting fifteen months that charted most of New Zealand and accomplished the most significant feat of Cook's first voyage, in discovering and coasting the east coast of Australia, thus establishing the existence of that continent and adding it to the British empire.

Tupaia is credited by all writers who are concerned with Polynesian voyaging with having drawn the famous "Tupaia's Map." The original, oddly enough, has been lost, and there remains only a "copy" drawn by Cook. I am convinced that Tupaia himself never set pen or pencil to paper to draw this or any other map; no Polynesian ever made any literal graphic representations, nor ever conceived of a map. It was Cook, I believe, who transposed Tupaia's oral and gestural directions to paper. And between the two of them, the map became a classic document.

Here is a somewhat abbreviated quotation of Beaglehole's comment on Tupaia's Chart. "This list [of the names on the chart] is not altogether hopeless as [Capt. W. J. L.] Wharton roundly declares, but as a guide to the Pacific it certainly leaves something to be desired. It is complicated not merely by the fact that Cook was reducing a strange language to writing, and running prefixes into names, but by the further facts that some of the names are evidently ancient ones and not now used, and that the directions in which they lie are sometimes considerably out —either because of erroneous information from Tupaia or because his information was misunderstood. At the same time one must remember that quite different islands often had identical names. It is possible to identify, either certainly, or to the point of near certainty, between forty and fifty, and close study by a deep Polynesian scholar would probably make fairly good sense of the whole list [73]."

The Raiatean version according to Teuira Henry is even more "distorted" because the whole Temehani is submerged and yet the little islet, Ro'o's refuge, remains dry in what must have been a vortex of water 3000 feet deep.

Another "wonder" as recounted by that most prolific of all recorders of Polynesian lore, Abraham Fornander, might alternately be entitled *Raiatea as Ararat*:

"At Raiatea, Society group, the legend runs that one day *Rua-Haku*, the Lord Rua, the Ocean God, was asleep at the bottom of the sea, when a fisherman came along that way with his hook and line. The hook got entangled in the hair of the god, and the fisherman, thinking he had caught a fine fish on his hook, pulled up so vigorously as to bring the god to the surface. Enraged at being thus disturbed in his sleep, the god threatened instant destruction to the unlucky fisherman; but the latter, having implored the god's pardon, was told to repair to a coral bank or islet called *Toa-marama* for shelter, while the god vented his displeasure on the rest of the world. The fisherman did as he was told, and took a friend, a hog, a dog, and a couple of hens with him to the islet. After that the ocean commenced rising, and continued rising until all the land was covered with water and all the people had perished. Then the waters retired, and the fisherman returned to his former home. Other versions of the event exist at Tahiti, but equally distorted."

Perhaps this is the canoe shed mentioned by Joseph Banks on page 140. The British Museum notes cautiously that the drawing is "unsigned," but it seems in the style of Parkinson and is entitled in his writing "View in Ulietea."

Its coconut tree is an interesting one with its large, ripe nuts, its small green nuts, and the flower stems below, ready to produce anew. He had, I would say, a botanist's eye. A mature tree

Before we come to the missionaries, or firstly to the discoverers who preceded them, I would like to call attention to one more of Raiatea's outstanding talents, one that is perhaps, dearest of all to my heart: canoe building. There is ample evidence that it was the Raiateans who, among all the islanders, were the master builders of canoes. Cook writes of "one of the largest double canoes I have any where seen . . . built to row with 144 paddles and capable to carrying a far greater number of men." (He is probably referring to a war canoe.) It was most likely the Raiateans who built the great double canoes that took the sailors of these central islands (by then generally known as Tahitians, as they and their language are still known today) to Hawaii and to the Cooks and to New Zealand. The crews were all called Tahitians, but you may be certain that since Raiateans built the canoes, they also, to some extent at least (and probably to a large one), manned and navigated them.

On the mountain slopes of Raiatea grew the finest great breadfruit trees, mara trees, and hutu trees. These were felled by stone adzes, dragged down carefully to the shore, set under a high, wide shed, and fashioned and hollowed out to form the essential keel members of each canoe. The sides were then built up, from wide boards split by wedges from large logs. After this the boards were trimmed to fit and were laced in place with taut coconut fibers. But pictures will serve better than words.

The canoe was the basic foundation piece of Polynesian society. It brought the settlers here from Samoa in the first place, and it spread them thence to all three corners of the huge oceanic triangle. Because it demanded the highest skill and the greatest physical stamina of its crews, it also acted as a rigorous selective agent of the

will bear as many as 100 nuts a year. *Cocos nucifera* will start bearing in 5 or 6 years, will bear well for 60 years and live on at a slower rate for a century.

A hundred nuts a year for 54 years plus an average of 70 nuts for another 40 years makes a total of 8 or 10 thousand in a tree's lifetime. Is there any individual producer anywhere, animal or vegetable, to match it?

The hull of a canoe in the making sketched by Webber. It seems an almost perfect representation of the one Banks describes on page 141, but it is unlikely to be the same vessel because Webber was on Cook's third voyage some eight years later. It may remind you however of how consistent the traditions of canoe building were then and probably had been for a couple of thousand years.

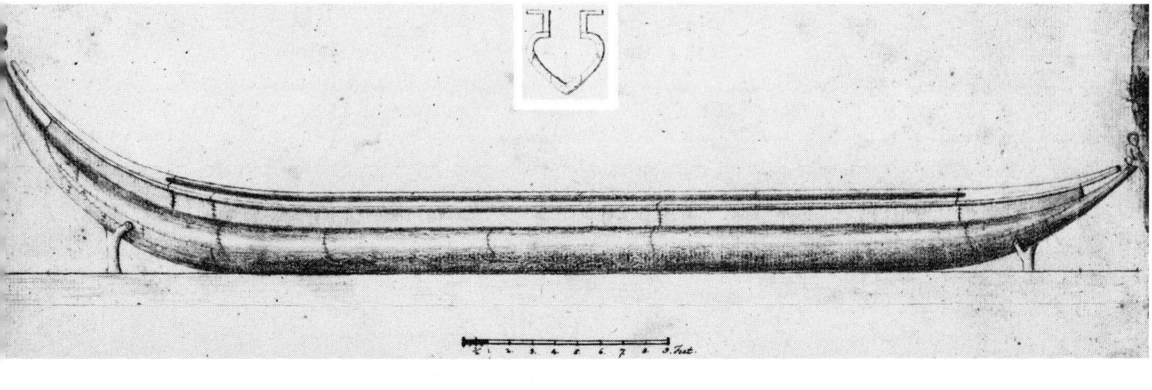

William Hodges, Cook's artist on his second voyage, 1772–1775, shows us first a splendid array of war canoes and then a good selection of workaday double-hull and outrigger craft.

Parkinson's double canoe on page 133 is a gay rendition of everyday life on our Raiatean lagoon with Tahaa in the background.

gene pools that were to grow into new civilizations on new island groups. It was, moreover, of basic religious importance: a canoe was the cradle to receive a newborn child and a coffin for his ultimate corpse.

There were many varieties of this noble vessel, ranging from the double-hulled ocean cruisers, commonly 60 to 80 feet long, up to war canoes of well over 100 feet, and down to smaller double canoes that were the numerous all-purpose carriers (some 20 to 40 feet in length) and to the multitude of single-hull outrigger canoes for fishing and transport of freight and passengers within and without the lagoons (lone-passenger hulls running from ten feet to longer ones of 25 or 30 feet), as well as larger, racing canoes holding twenty or so paddlers. (Sometimes the

smaller racers flew a huge kite, to skim them before a fair breeze in the manner of our modern-day "planing.") The general name "canoe" for all of these ingenious vessels is surely a misnomer, one applied by Europeans who had learned it from the American Indian's fresh-water, birch-bark craft and applied it indiscriminately to all hollowed-out means of floating transportation, wherever he found them anywhere in the world. But the Polynesians had different names for all of their different types, pahi, va'a, tipaeama, tipaeati, tahifa, taurua, etc.

What a superb invention is the canoe! Almost as significant and perhaps even more ancient than, the wheel. What the wheel did on land, the canoe did on water. It got man up on the surface and sped him, with a fraction of his previous effort, to wherever he wanted to go. It would be tempting to say that the Polynesian invented the canoe, but as a race he is far too young for that. However, there is no question that he brought it in his twin-hulled, deep-sea sailing form to its ultimate versatility and perfection, well beyond that achieved by any of the other cultures of man. And therefore can't the Raiatean be proud that his canoes were the very best of all?

But for a drawing of a big blue-water double canoe there is none, according to our foremost expert and most respected authority, James Hornell, to surpass this wash drawing by Webber. He gives us no scale but if we assume the deckhouse to be about six feet high at the peak (these houses were built low, to sit in and sleep in, and also to avoid windage), the hulls are some 60 feet and the whole is 96 feet overall. Quite a vessel!

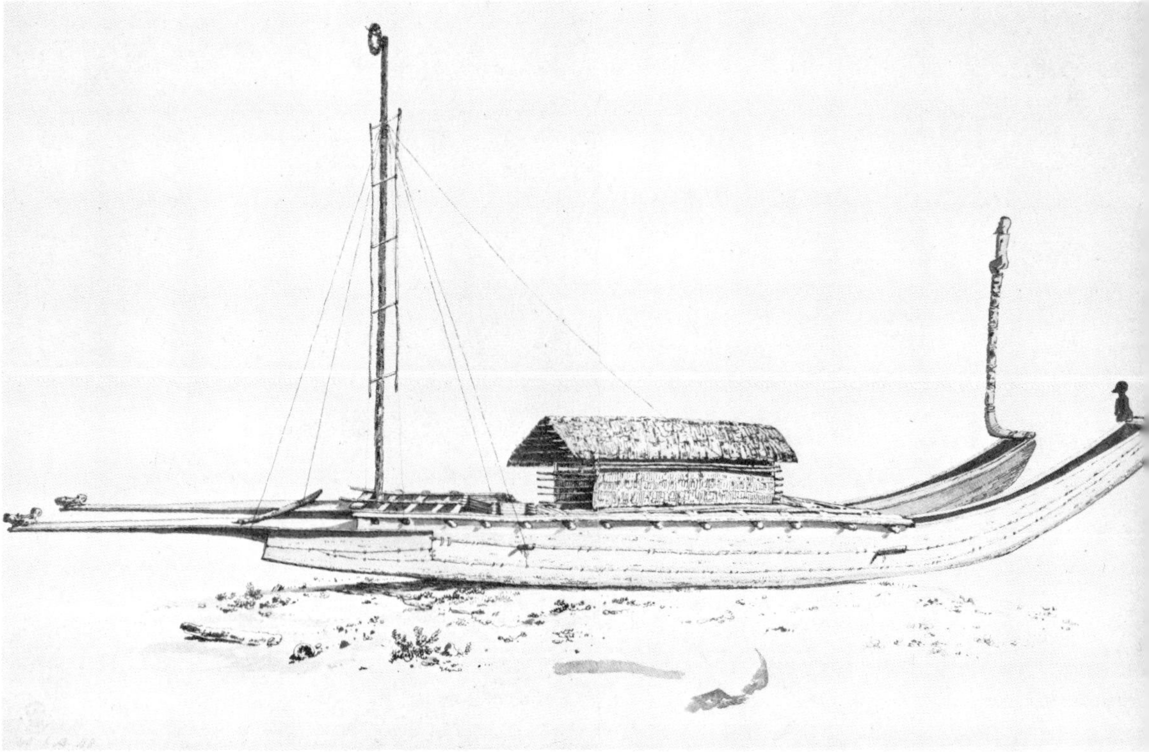

CHAPTER SEVEN

The White Man Cometh

We have now surveyed geologic and botanical accounts of the origins of Raiatea as conceived by modern science, and its mythological origins according to ancient Polynesian lore. And we have also reviewed man's first coming and impressions of the culture developed there before the missionaries came to overthrow it. Actually the arrivals of the European discoverers constitute an ominous, though less disastrous, prelude to the coming of the missionaries. (Orders typical of those given to each group upon setting out from home will be found in the Appendix.)

Wallis is credited with having been the first to set foot on Tahiti, in 1767, though some claim that the famous Spanish navigator, Quiros, sighted the island in 1606. The

This engraving of the dramatic attack by the Tahitians on Wallis's *Dolphin* is, like Hawkesworth's dancers, another secondhand rendition by a stay-at-home artist and full of such errors as the main double canoe being paddled stern first. The reason for including it here is to point out that the first visitors from Europe were by no means wholly welcome. The natives were disarmingly friendly at first, but after a few days a large fleet of canoes suddenly materialized and the Englishmen were subjected to a fierce hail of slingstones. Only cannon saved them. Reprisals were cruel.

A Representation of The ATTACK on CAPT.N WALLIS in the DOLPHIN, by the Natives of OTAHEITE.

This portrait of James Cook by Nathaniel Dance is generally considered the best likeness at the height of his fame.

Spaniards, however, were notoriously secretive about all of their discoveries because they wanted all new lands for themselves and to be unknown to others. Moreover, their records, such as have subsequently been ferreted out, show discrepancies in identification that make a sighting of Tahiti suspect. So let us grant that Wallis was the first. But he never saw Raiatea, nor did the second European to visit the neighborhood, Louis de Bougainville in 1768.

Our holy little island was thus reserved for Captain James Cook, who sailed to the leeward islands of the Society group after making his celebrated observation of the transit of Venus in Tahiti in 1769. His stay was short, only eleven days, and many of them he spent on board ship because of bad weather. Here is the typically, matter of fact account of the first landing of the white man on Raiatea.

"Thursday 20th. Moderate breezes at East and ENE

fair weather. At ½ past 2 PM weigh'd and made sail for the Island of Ulietea which lies SWBW distant 7 or 8 Leagues from Huahiene, at ½ past 6 we were within 3 Leagues of it, then shortened sail and Stood off and on all night, and at day light made sail in shore and soon after discover'd an opening in the reef that lies along this side of the Island within which Tupia said was a good harbr. Upon this I hoisted out the Pinnace and sent the Master in to examine it who soon made the signal for the ship to follow, accordingly we stood in and anchor'd in 22 fathom soft ground: soon after we anchor'd some of the Natives came on board the Ship with very little invatation.

"Friday 21st July. Winds variable and dark clowdy weather with frequent Showers of rain. At 1 PM I landed in company with Mr. Banks and the other Gentlemen, the first thing done was the performing of Tupia's ceremony in all respects as at Huaheine. I then hoisted an English Jack and took possession of the Island & those adjacent in the name of His Britk Majestys, calling them by the same names as the Natives do."

H.M.S. *Endeavour Bark* (from an original watercolor by Richard Linton).

Later on in his *Journal* Cook does recollect that "The people of this island are in general far more superstitious [i.e. religious] than at Otaheite or any of the other isles." He also found them "the most obligeing and benevolent people I ever met with."

Joseph Banks was more inquisitive and, to us, more interesting. Again with footnotes by Beaglehole, he records:

"At noon today come to an anchor at *Ulhietea* in a bay Calld by the natives *Oapoa*[1] the entrance of which is very near a small Islet Calld *Owhattera.*[2] Some Indians soon came on board expressing signs of fear, they were two Canoes each of which brought a woman, I suppose as a mark of confidence, and a pig as a present. To each of these ladies was given a spike nail and some beads with which they seemed much pleased. Tupia who has always expressed much fear of the men of *Bola Bola*[3] says that they have conquered this Island and will tomorrow come down and fight with us, we therefore lose no time in going ashore as we are to have today to ourselves. On landing Tupia repeated the ceremony of praying as at Huahine after which an English Jack was set up on shore and Captn Cooke took possession of this and the other three Islands in sight viz. *Huahine Otahah*[4] and *Bola Bola* for the use of his Britannick majesty. After this we walk together to a great *Marai* calld *Tapodeboatea* whatever that may signifie;[5] it is different from those of Otahite being no

[1] Opoa.

[2] Oatara.

[3] Porapora (more properly) or Borabora (as spelt today).

[4] Tahaa, Raiatea and Tahaa are enclosed by the same reef.

[5] Taputapu-atea, Banks's spelling shows the ambiguity between the Tahitian *t* and *d* sounds. S has the note, 'Tapodeboatea. Signifies in their Language, Head of the white Hog'. This is an unhappy bloomer on Banks's part; perhaps he gets it out of *Te upoo* (the human head) + *te puaa* (the hog) + *tea* (white). Henry (*Ancient Tahiti*, p. 95) gives its meaning as 'Sacrifices from abroad'. *Taputapu* was a sacrifice, generally human, to the god Oro; one of the meanings of *atea* was 'distant, far off'. Davies defines the word as 'the name of a public and principal heiva, where the human sacrifices were made to Oro'. Such sacrifices were made at other *marae* in Tahiti named after this one. It was the most famous of all *marae*, and of international significance, as the most important *marae* of Raiatea, the centre from which the Society Islands and Tahiti were populated, and the homeland to which the Maori people trace back their historic origin. Emory (op.cit., pp. 145-8) has a full discussion of the *marae*, with drawings.

Let us, all Polynesiophiles, send up a paen of praise to J. C. Beaglehole, that stalwart New Zealand scholar who annotated and indexed the massive journals of Captain Cook and Joseph Banks in such an imaginative and utterly thorough way that they spring alive again after two hundred years and, indeed, take on a new life that, save for him, never would have come so pleasantly to pass.

This portrait of Sir Joseph Banks painted by Sir Joshua Reynolds shows him as a young man perhaps before he was knighted and president of the Royal Society (after which our Society Islands were named). This was probably painted shortly after his return from Cook's first voyage. A gentleman of considerable means, an accomplished botanist and adventurous explorer, he added greatly to the public glamour of Cook's first circumnavigation, but when the second voyage was outfitting, his demands for accommodations for his many companions and servants were so extravagant that Cook ripped off the unseaworthy superstructure that had been built to provide extra quarters and left Sir Joseph at home in a huff.

more than walls about 8 feet high of Coral Stones (s of an immense size) filld up with smaller ones, the w ornamented with many planks set upon their ends and c their whole lengh. In the neighbourhood of this we fo the altar or *ewhatta*[6] upon which lay the last sacrific hog of about 80 pounds weight which had been put there whole and very nicely roasted. Here were also 4 5 *Ewharre no Eatua* or god houses which were made to carried on poles. One of these I examind by putting hand into it: within was a parsel about 5 feet long and c thick wrappd up in matts, these I tore with my fingers I came to a covering of mat made of platted Cocoa n fibres which it was impossible to get through so I was

[6] *fata*; Banks again includes the verbal *e*, it is.

obligd to desist, especialy as what I had already done gave much offence to our new friends.[7] From hence we went to an adjoining long house where among several things such as rolls of cloth &c. was standing a model of a Canoe about 3 feet long upon which were tied 8 under jaw bones of men. Tupia told us that it was the custom of these Islanders to cut off the Jaw bones of those who they had killd in war; these were he said the jaw bones of Ulhietea people but how they came here or why tied thus to a canoe we could not understand, we were therefore contented to conjecture that they were plac'd there as a trophy won back from the men of Bola Bola their mortal enemies. Night now came on apace but Dr Solander and myself walkd along shore a little way and saw an *Ewharre no Eatua*, the under part of which was lind with a row of Jaw bones which we were also told were those of Ulhietea men. We saw also Cocoa nut trees the stemms of which were hung around with nutts so that no part of them could be seen, these we were told were put there that they might dry a little and be prepard for making *poe*; we saw also a tree of *Ficus prolixa* in great perfection, the trunck or rather congeries of roots of which was 42 paces in circumference.[8]

"21. Dr Solander and myself walkd out this morn and saw many large boathouses like that describd at Huahine page 303 and 401.[9] On these the inhabitants were at work making and repairing the large Canoes calld by them *Pahee*,[10] at which business they workd with incredible cleverness tho their tools certainly were as bad as possible. I will first give the dimensions and description of one of their boats

Hutu

[7] Not surprisingly; and it is a tribute to Raiatean tolerance that they remained the young man's friends after this calm piece of sacrilege. The object which Banks was trying to get at was a sennit representation of an ancestral god, perhaps the great god Oro, to whom the *marae* was sacred.

[8] *Ficus prolixa* Forst., called Aoa by the Tahitians, was a sacred tree planted about temples, its 'congeries of roots' like a banyan; its bark was used in making *tapa* cloth. Solander provided a full description both of this and of *F. tinctoria* (*Prim. Fl. Insul. Oceani Pac.* pp. 352-3 MS) but Forster in true form purloined Solander's names for his *Prodromus* (cf. Merrill, p. 352).

[9] i.e. pp. 316 above, and 368 below.

[10] *pahi.* The people of Raiatea were the great canoe-builders of the Society group. The description which Banks proceeds to give is more detailed than anything in Cook.

and then their methód of building. Its extreme lenght from stem to stern not reckoning the bending up of both those parts 51 feet; breadth in the clear at the top forward 14 inches, midships 18, aft 15; in the bilge forward 32 inches, midships 35, aft 33; depth midships 3 ft 4; hight from the ground she stood on 3 ft 6; hęr head raisd without the figure 4 ft 4 from the ground, the figure 11 inches; her stern 8 ft 9, the figure 2 feet. Alongside of her was lashd another like her in all parts but less in proportion being only 33 feet in her extreme lengh. The form of these Canoes is better to be expressd by a drawing than by any description. This annexd may serve to give some Idea of a section: *aa* is the first seam, *bb* the second, *cc* the third. The first stage or keel under *aa* is made of trees hollowd out like a trough for which purpose they chuse the longest trees they can get,[11] so that 2 or three make the bottom of their largest boats (some of which are much larger than that describd here as I make a rule to describe every thing of this kind from the common size); the next stage under *bb* is formd of streght plank about 4 feet long and 15 inches broad and 2 inches thick; the next stage under *cc* is made like the bottom of trunks of trees hollowd into its bilging form; the last or that above *cc* is formd also out of trunks of trees so that the moulding is of one peice with the plank. This work dificult as it would be to an Europæan with his Iron tools they perform without Iron and with amazing dexterity; they hollow with their stone axes as fast at least as our Carpenters could do and dubb tho slowly with prodigious nicety; I have seen them take off a skin of an angular plank without missing a stroke, the skin itself scarce 1/16 part of an inch in thickness. Boring the holes throug[h] which their sewing is to pass seems to be their greatest dificulty. Their tools are made of the bones of men, generaly the thin bone of the upper arm; these they grind

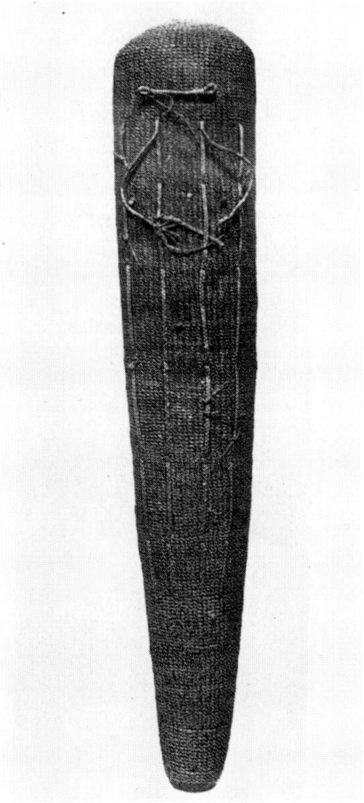

Faifai

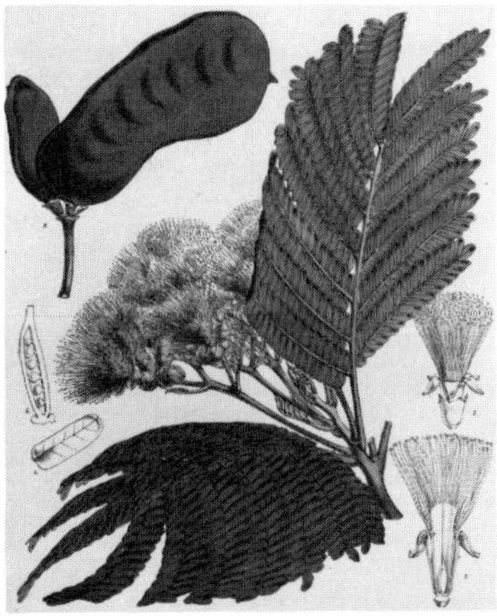

[11] The timbers used for canoe-building were mainly Faifai (*Serianthes myriadenia*) a large valley-growing tree, a favourite for *pahi*; the Uru or breadfruit, and the Hutu (*Barringtonia speciosa*)—for which last see Pl. V.

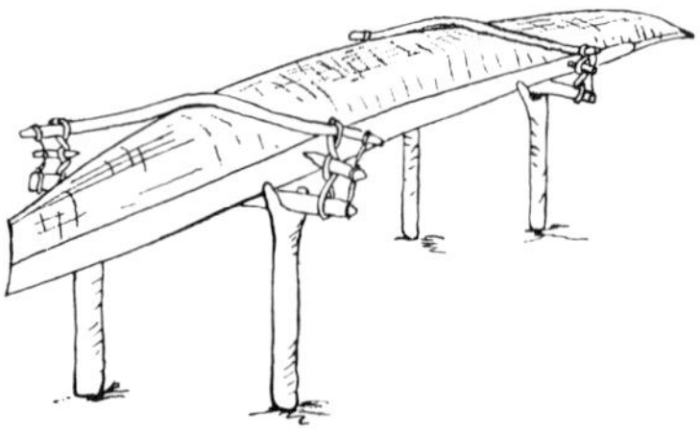

very sharp and fix to a handle of wood, making the instrument serve the purpose of a gouge by striking it with a mallet made of a hard black wood,[12] and with them would do as much work as with Iron tools was it not that the brittle Edge of the tool is very liable to be broke.

"When they have prepard their planks &c. the keel is layd on blocks and the whole Canoe put together much in the same manner as we do a ship, the sides being supported by stantions and all the seams wedg'd together before the last sewing is put on, so that they become tolerably tight considering that they are without calking.[13]

"With these boats they venture themselves out of sight of land; we saw several of them at Otahite which had come from Ulhietea and Tupia has told us that they go voyages of twenty days, whether true or false I do not affirm. They keep them very carefully under such boat-houses as are describd p.   , one of which we measurd today 60 yards by 11."

Later on in his journal Mr. Banks comments on the Arioi. He is worth quoting, for he is probably the first European to have encountered our famous players on their native soil:

"One amusement more I must mention tho I confess I hardly dare touch upon it as it is founded upon a custom so devilish, inhuman, and contrary to the first principles of human nature that tho the natives have repeatedly told it to me, far from concealing it rather looking upon it as a branch of freedom upon which they valued themselves, I can hardly bring myself to believe it much less expect that any body Else shall. It is this that more than half of the better sort of the inhabitants of the Island have like Comus in Milton enterd into a resolution of enjoying free liberty in love without a possibility of being troubled or disturbd by its consequences; these mix together with the utmost freedom seldom cohabiting together more than one or two days by which means they have fewer children than they would otherwise have, but those who are so unfortunate

[12] Toa or ironwood.

[13] This is evidently a mistake. Caulking was done with fine coconut fibre and the adhesive sap of the breadfruit used as pitch; but Banks probably did not see the process.

This "Young Woman . . . bringing a Present" may not be an Arioi, but perhaps she is bringing presents to them, for they were plied lavishly wherever they went with all the wealth of the land, such as these two pearl-shell and feather gorgets, much prized as gifts. Whoever she is, she is here simply because she is beguiling as engraved for Cook's *Atlas* from a wash drawing by Webber. Incidentally, although the engraving is otherwise faithful to the original, in Webber's painting the maiden's right breast is covered. It was evidently the engraver's conceit to do a bit of discreet stripteasing.

as to be thus begot are smotherd at the moment of their birth. Some of these people have been pointed out to me by name and on being askd have not denyd the fact, who have contracted intimacies and livd together for years and even now continue to do so, in the course of which 2, 3 or more children have been born and destroyd.

"They are calld *Arreoy* and have meetings among themselves where the men amuse themselves with wrestling &c. and the women with dancing the indecent dances before mentiond,[1] in the course of which they give full liberty to their desires but I beleive keep strictly up to the appearances of decency. I never was admitted to see them,

[1] There appears to be no single word corresponding to this. Obviously the dance was a matter of light-hearted erotic amusement. The phrases *te ai moro-iti* or *ti moro-iti* would mean copulation or a sort of pseudo-copulation. Parkinson, p. 61, gives the meaning of 'Taimoradee' as 'To reel to and fro'.

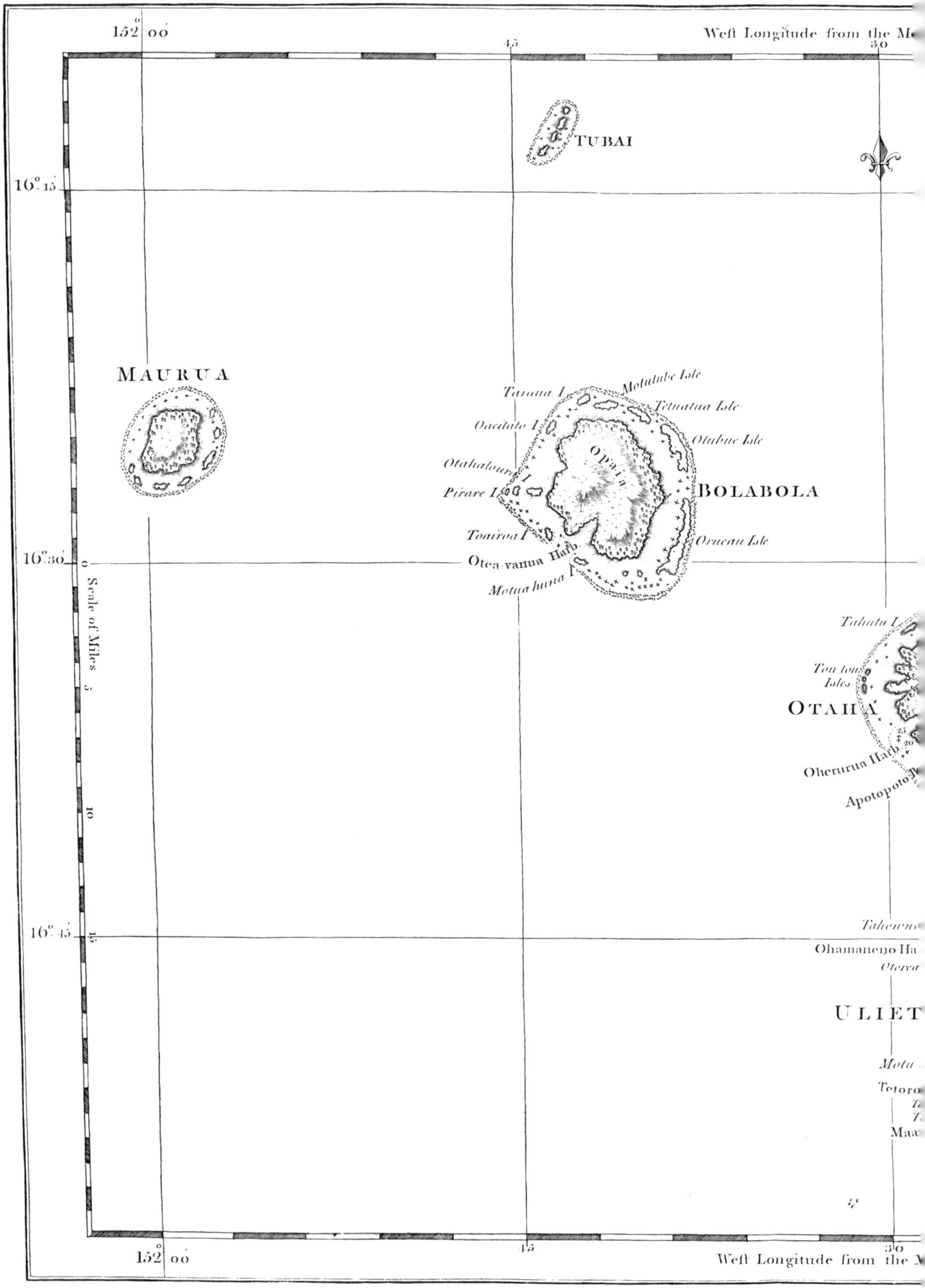

152° 00'
45
West Longitude from the M
30
TUBAI
16°.15'
MAURUA
Tanaua I.
Motutube Isle
Tetuatua Isle
Oacitato I.
Otubue Isle
Opaia
Otahalour I.
Pirare I.
BOLABOLA
Toairoa I.
Orueau Isle
16°.30'
Otea-vanua Harb.
Motua huna I.
Scale of Miles
0
5
10
15
Tahuta I.
Tou tou Isles
OTAHA
Oherurua Harb.
Apotopoto
16°.45'
Ohamaneno Ha
ULIET
Tetoro
Maa
152° 00'
45
30
West Longitude from the

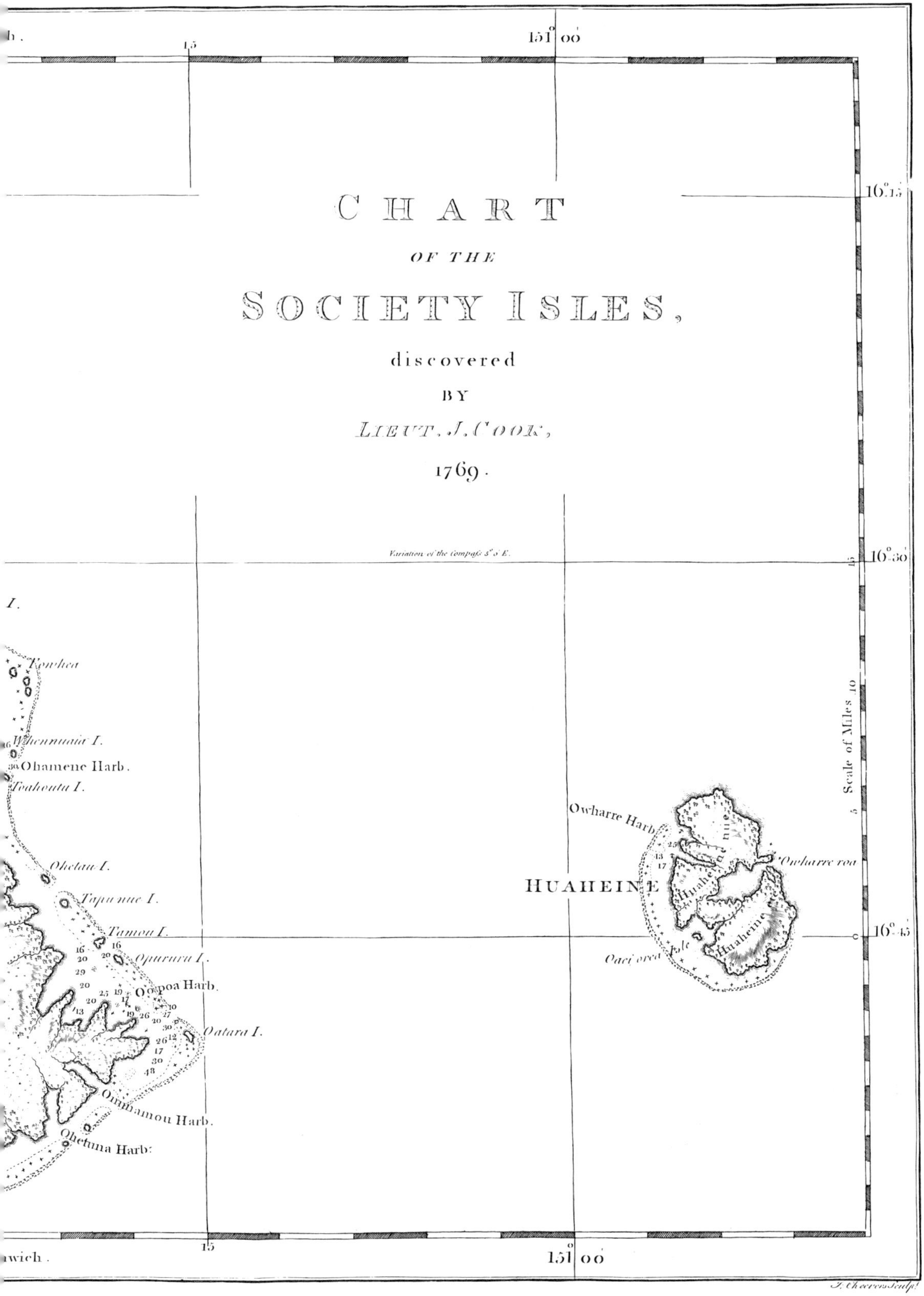

CHART
OF THE
SOCIETY ISLES,
discovered
BY
LIEUT. J. COOK,
1769.
Variation of the Compass 5° 0' E.
151° 00'
15
16° 15'
16° 30'
16° 45'
Scale of Miles
Towhea
Whennuaia I.
Ohamene Harb.
Toahoutu I.
Ohetau I.
Tapu nue I.
Tamou I.
Opururu I.
Oopoa Harb.
Oatara I.
Ommamou Harb.
Ohetuna Harb.
HUAHEINE
Owharre Harb.
Owharre roa
Huaheine nue
Huaheine iti
Oaci orea
J. Cheevers Sculp.

one of our gentlemen saw part of one but I beleive very little of their real behavior tho he saw enough to make him give credit to what we had been told.

"This custom as indeed it is natural to suppose Owes as we were told its existence cheifly to the men. A Woman howsoever fond she may be of the name of Arreoy and the liberty attending it before she conceives, generaly desires much to forfeit that title for the preservation of her child: in this she has not the smallest influence; if she cannot find a man who will own it she must of course destroy it; and if she can, with him alone it lies whether or not it shall be preserv'd: sometimes it is, but in that case both the man and woman forfeit their title of Arreoy and the privelege annext thereunto, and must for the future be known by the term *Whannownow*,[2] or bearer of children: a title as disgracefull among these people as it ought to be honourable in every good and well governd society. In this case the man and woman generaly live together as man and wife for the remainder of their lives.[3]"

[2] *fanaunau*, degraded.

[3] Banks's account of the *arioi*, that famous society, is true as far as it goes, but naturally enough it does not go very far. They were a society fairly widely-spread in Polynesia, though founded too late to be brought to New Zealand; with functions both secular and religious—if the two can be really separated, in a social system so thoroughly interpenetrated with religion. They were the great actors of ritual, and for the islands the opera, drama and dance rolled into one. The infanticide which was so widely practised seems to have been both an aid to what might be called celibacy, so advantageous to public performers, constantly on the move, and a measure of population-control; for in an island economy increase always brought considerable problems. It was natural therefore that the *arioi* should have divine origin and sanctions, and elaborate gradations and ceremonial observances of their own. Obviously they represented the erotic side of life, but as we have seen, their functions were much wider than that. Purea, Amo, Tupaia (to take only three examples) were all *arioi*.

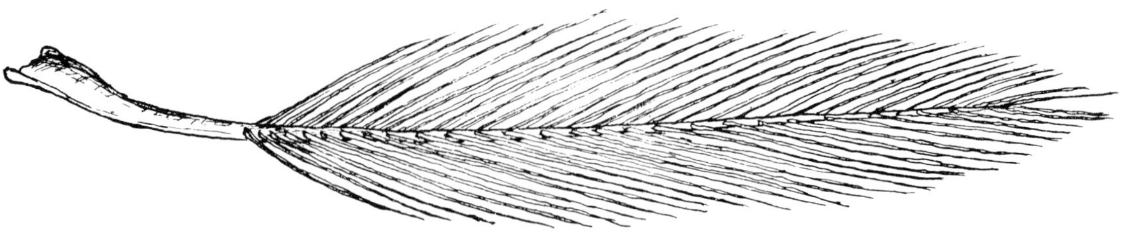

A View near Ohamaneno Harbour in Ulietea.

So much, then, for the explorers. Although a number of others touched at Raiatea, notably Vancouver, they write almost exclusively of Tahiti and treat our island as a mere satellite. After them came traders and whalers, but they, too, rarely and only casually touched at Raiatea. Tahiti was their prime objective, the first and ideal stopping place to recover from scurvy and other ailments of their long voyages around the Horn, to reprovision, to regale themselves with feminine hospitality, and to leave with the natives venereal and other decimating diseases.

Before these scourges had, however, wrought their well-known, lethal, physical effects the missionaries had come, zealously to rend and almost totally destroy the lovely fabric of the native culture. It is sad indeed to reflect on the cultural corruption that was being spread throughout the world by militant Christianity. But those who brought "enlightenment" were good men. They knew not what they did, but they did it with the highest of purpose and most righteous intent. Take, for instance, one of the earliest and most picturesque of them, the Reverend Orsmond. It is to him we owe by far the greater part of the

The title of this charming little scene is "A View near Ohamaneno Harbour in Ulietea" and the British Library tells us that it is "by Captain Cook probably copied from one of the artists on the first voyage." This is the harbor on the southwest coast right around from us at Fetuna, where Cook repaired several times on his second and third voyages. It was the home of the high chief Orea, father of the famous Poetua. The dwelling seems too humble for a great chief and yet the private homes of the arii were often no more sumptuous than those of relatively well-off landowners. It might perhaps have been "our house" where Cook's astronomer, William Wales, says (on page 123) that "Chastity . . . was not seemingly considered as one of the Cardinal Virtues."

The drawing is almost identical to one by Parkinson entitled "Home and Plantation of a chief of the Island of

Otaheite" and if Cook copied it from Parkinson, it would be an example of how casual these gentlemen sometimes were about inconsequential locations and minor details. The two dwellings may have been so similar that an exact rendering of their differences was deemed unimportant. Of course most of these drawings and washes were first sketched roughly in the field, then finished off on shipboard on the voyage home or in London after arrival. Memories and notes are understandably not always exact.

Captain Wilson

legendary and mythical material in this book. He was profoundly convinced that these people were heathen and that their ways were evil. He strove mightily to eradicate their pernicious customs, but he recorded them all faithfully and voluminously—and thereby hangs a tale.

John Muggeridge Orsmond was born in a country town in England about 1784. He trained for the ministry and, as soon as he was ordained, decided he wanted to be a missionary. It was a glamorous prospect in those empire-building, colonizing, pre-Victorian days of good King George whom the thirteen American colonies had just rejected. The London Missionary Society had recently started up and was dispatching its disciples to all corners of the heathen earth. (One would hesitate to say their chief aim was to get to those corners ahead of the Catholics, but one can't help wondering.)

The first contingent of missionaries to the Pacific, 30 of them, with six wives and three children, was sent in 1796 on a ship chartered especially for that purpose by the Society, the *Duff*, under the command of a pious sea captain named James Wilson. It dropped off missionaries as it sailed from island group to island group, even in the process discovering some new islands. Since the natives were not always friendly, most of the brethern were settled in the Tahitian or Tongan islands. One unfortunate fellow named John Harris, who dared the Marquesas, was an object of great curiosity to the ladies of what he hoped would become his parish. His long gowns made him look to them more like a woman than a man. Moreover, he resisted sternly all of their amourous wiles and advances. Then, one night a few of them stole into his hut and sent their inquiring fingers under his robe, to feel the answer to their puzzlement. The poor man shrieked in horror and took the next boat home.

Of all glamorous prospects in those days following the voyages of Wallis, Bougainville, and Cook, Tahiti was a natural choice, and with that destination in view, young Reverend Orsmond and his newly acquired wife set sail on a convict ship for Australia. It was evidently an exciting voyage, for there was a brush with Algerian pirates, a fire on board, and a mutiny of the convicts before they

This detail (about one half the whole plate) from Captain Wilson's book shows the good ship *Duff* in Oponuhu bay in Moorea. Above her to the left towers Mount Rotui, which Tafai climbed in vain to catch the spirit of his beloved Hina before it parted for the rendezvous on the Temehani.

reached Sydney in 1817. Meanwhile, during the long days at sea, the Reverend Orsmond had devoted his considerable energies and good sense to the learning of the Tahitian language from several natives who were fellow passengers. By the time he reached Moorea, in April of the same year, he could converse well, and soon he mastered the language. (J. Frank Stimson tells us this, and he himself was a master linguist.) This fluency in the native speech was, of course, of primary importance. It is an objective that seems obvious enough in these days of the anthropologist, but in those times it was, alas, seldom appreciated. The chief concern was to make *them* learn *our* language. Indeed, such a view persists even today. For example, throughout the central Polynesian islands the French have established a very efficient school system housed in modern well-appointed buildings, in which hour after hour, day after day only the French language is spoken or written. Moreover, it is taught from textbooks and readers that take little Polynesians down elevators to shop in supermarkets and to wander through parks in baby carriages. The Polynesian kids learn readily enough, for they are bright and they are obliging, but they never speak French to each other out of school and, as soon as the compulsory grades are ground through in their late teens, they quickly relegate the Gallic language to occasional dealings with tourists or to business matters. If this seems incredible to us in this day and age, consider the nun whom we met in the Marquesas. This dedicated sister had spent 28 years living amongst and caring for her flock, yet she had never bothered to learn to speak their language.

Reverend Orsmond fortunately had a prescience of the anthropologist in him. He not only learned the language in order to convert the heathen, save their souls, and bring them the blessed revelations of the true Gospel, he also took patient care to record their own gospels: their chants, legends, traditions, genealogies. He learned them from all ranks—chiefs, priests, *arioi*, landed gentry, and manahune. He took them down in writing as they spoke. He recorded them endlessly in many variations. He had an appreciation, which is rare, of the disadvantages of literacy, in contrast to the advantages of purely oral communication. A written language requires a very extensive, always increasing vocabulary. An oral language, like music, can achieve a wide range of forms and meanings with only a handful of elements. The literate man is tied to his written alphabet. When he encounters the illiterate man and attempts to set down on paper what has been said, he finds he must spell the same way, in the same letters, a word that has twenty different meanings and shades of meaning, ranging from black to white and hate to love and yes to no. In Davies's dictionary the word ao, for instance, has 23 definitions. Here is a sampling of them: day, the light, a hospitable man, the opening buds of trees, the name of a large sea bird, grooves of the cloth mallet, the fat of turtles, braided human hair, a sail rope, a spy that comes upon a party at night, to press the liquid out of a strainer, to peep as an eel out of its hole, counsel, warning, reproof.

In Davies's history of the Tahitian Mission he describes the difficulties the brethren encountered in this regard:

"Our growth in the knowledge of the language is still slow and in many cases uncertain; which is in great measure owing, to our not being able to catch the sound of the words, with that exactness that is necessary. The language abounds with vowels, even more than any navigator who has given specimens of it was aware. Many words consist of nothing but vowels, and each has a sound; but the natives utter their words with such rapidity, that it is with the utmost difficulty we can discover the true manner of spelling them: and when this is accomplished with any tolerable degree of precision, there is as great a labour to arrive at the true sense and meaning of a word, or its various meanings; for one word is used to express very opposite things in different sentences; and, which adds to the difficulty, they abbreviate words so much, that those which we are well acquainted with, and which, if fully pronounced we should readily understand, are by the abbreviation so shortened, that we frequently mistake them for new words, and are thus puzzled and perplexed."

The word aue ranges from joy to despair, acceptance to rejection. There is no real "yes" in Polynesia, only the

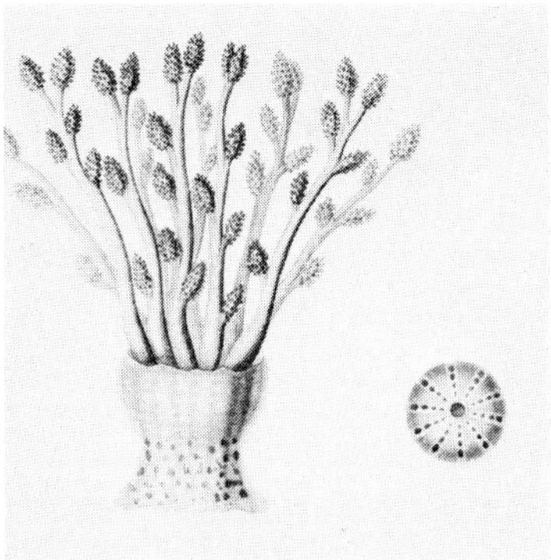

expletive E, meaning "I understand" or "I have heard you" (but not necessarily denoting agreement). But the Polynesian "no," aita, has a thousand negative meanings, depending on how it is uttered. All of these depend on the music of the word, how it is said, when it is said, the context in which it is said, even the conditions in which it is *not* said, but implied, to this intention or to that. How can such a word be spelled? Impossible; and yet how easily it can be spoken, especially when accompanied by a gesture of the hand, a grimace, a smile, or a twinkle of the eye. And how do you spell those? No, the richness and sublety of the old Polynesian language cannot be recorded, especially not on paper.

Reverend Orsmond also worked on the dictionary that the missionaries were preparing for the London Missionary Society. Indeed, Frank Stimson feels that Orsmond was the chief architect of that most valuable work. When it was finally published, after many long delays, in 1851, it was attributed to the Reverend John Davies, "with the assistance of D. Darling." But by that time the Reverend Orsmond had been expelled from the London Missionary Society. (For many years the brethren in the Tahitian islands had been sensing, with alarm, the increasing penetration of French military [and Catholic] power. It had been dismaying the Tahitians as well, and Queen Pomare had frequently appealed to Queen Victoria, offering to deliver the islands to the English in order to save them from the French. But the British were apparently too busy acquiring their pieces of empire elsewhere to be bothered with a packet of small, unexploitable islands in the middle of the Pacific. The Reverend Orsmond had the good sense to foresee the inevitable, and unlike his chauvanistic brethren, he decided to work with the French, rather than against them. He was, thus, branded as a traitor and evicted from the Society in 1844. He continued his work as a teacher probably just as effectively as ever, because of all the missionaries he was the most respected and loved. Later the French put him in charge of their Protestant mission. But most important to us, he continued his recording of native lore.)

The Reverend Orsmond was an indefatigable worker.

He not only preached, but he enforced, temperance. He built houses and churches in European style. He constructed roads and bridges. The learned and humane editor of his granddaughter's book at the Bishop Museum is anonymous, but his name was probably Edward S. Craighill Handy. He tells us that Orsmond did not hesitate to cut down breadfruit and coconut trees that grew in the villages because he felt an abundance of food too close to hand was conducive of sloth. Thus we see him a florid, driving, righteous bundle of energy, stirring up a placid, obliging populace, all for the sake of his own incomparable Jehovah. And yet at the same time he took the pains to make endless records of all of their own much less infallible, but much more colorful, jehovahs. He seems a curious paradox, but it is said that he mellowed his zeal considerably as he grew older, and his acceptance of the French conquest seems a tangible evidence of that.

The Reverend Orsmond says the boys "are more mannish here at 14 than boys in England at 17 or 19 & therefore less docile, the more impatient of restraint . . . I think I can say that there is not a little native creature who has reached his seventh year, but who knows more of human nature than I did at 28 years."

All along, while Reverend Orsmond was recording the traditional material, he was also editing and preparing it for publication. Finally, in 1848 he delivered his manuscript to the local French authorities headed by Commandant Lavaud, who in turn dispatched it to the Ministere des Colonies in Paris. And there it disappeared . . . forever.

Many a search has been made for it subsequently by scholars and officials, but not a trace of it has ever been found. Quatrefages in his book on Polynesian migrations, published in 1866, states that he examined some of Reverend Orsmond's material in conducting his research, manuscripts in the Reverend's own handwriting, but he says that the bulk of it had been lost. The Bishop Museum editor says it was probably burned, among other public documents circa 1848, during the advent of the Second French Republic. At any rate the Reverend Orsmond died in 1856 without learning anything of its fate. How heartbreaking for a lifetime's work and dedication.

Fortunately for us today, there is a not-unhappy sequel to this tale. Reverend Orsmond lost his first wife, Mary, and their infant child only a few years after their marriage. By his second wife, Isabella, he had a daughter who married the son of his fellow missionary, William Henry,

Teuira Henry

who had come to Tahiti even earlier than Orsmond, on the missionary ship *Duff* in 1797. These two, in turn, had a daughter whom they named Teuira; and Miss Henry, as she remained all her life, evidently discovered in herself a compulsive strain of her reverend grandfather. She became a schoolteacher in Papeete. She inherited all of her grandfather's massive hoard of papers, the original notes, observations, and recordings upon which his book had been based. She trained herself to become an accomplished linguist. This is of the greatest importance, because all of Reverend Orsmond's most valuable material was in archaic Tahitian, a language that had already been largely lost by the time Teuira took her task in hand and has now disappeared to such a degree that it is virtually impossible to correct or elaborate upon Teuira's text. And this is a pity because her published work, splendid as it is, could most probably be rendered much richer and more poetic if someone, Polynesian or expert linguist, could exhume it. Dr. Handy and Dr. Emory, who are the two men best qualified, indeed the only two who have the qualifications to come close to such a challenge, declare only that they are certain there are many possible meanings in addition to and in elaboration of the ones Teuira has chosen, but they know no way to find them.

Lest these final comments seem to cast a shadow on Teuira's book, it must be understood that, as I have said before, only a Polynesian Homer could have sung the real song. Moreover the unhappy fact that Teuira died before her work was completed prevented her from reviewing, revising, polishing—and even from correcting obvious typographical errors. So, we can only be thankful, very thankful, for the unique and bountiful wealth of her *Ancient Tahiti.* From it is gleaned almost all of the traditional substance of this little book on Raiatea, holy land of Polynesia.

There were a number of other observant missionaries, but none who took the pains, or developed the ability, to record so voluminously or meticulously as Orsmond. Davies's dictionary has been quoted, and it is an invaluable treasury of the old Tahitian language, but the primary purpose of its compilers was its use as a tool for converting the heathen.

Undoubtedly, the work most widely read at the time it was published was *Polynesian Researches* by William Ellis. While Orsmond's much finer book was delayed until 1928 and then was printed in a small quantity as a specialized bulletin of the Bishop Museum, Ellis's came out in two volumes in 1829 and was revised and reprinted in four volumes in 1834, 1853, and 1859. For the general reader Ellis is still the primary missionary source on early Polynesia. He spent nearly eight years in Polynesia, many of them on Raiatea. Here are a couple of passages, pertinent to our themes, that give a sampling of the man:

District of Opoa

"Raiatea is not only the most important island of the Leeward group, from its central situation and its geographical extent, but on account of its identity, in tradition, with the origin of the people, and their preservation in the general deluge. It has been distinguished as the cradle of their mythology, the birthplace and residence of Oro, the region to which disembodied spirits resorted, the seat of their oracle, and the abode of those priests whose predictions for many generations regulated the expectations of the nation. It is also intimately connected with the most important matters in the traditionary history and ancient religion of the people. *Opoa* is the most remarkable place in Raiatea; of its earth, according to some of their traditions, the first pair were made by Tii or Taaroa, and on its soil they fixed their abode. Here Oro held his court. It was called Hawaii; and as distant colonies are said to have proceeded from it, it was probably the place at which some of the first inhabitants of the South Sea Islands arrived. It has also long been a place of celebrity, not only in Raiatea, but throughout the whole of the So-

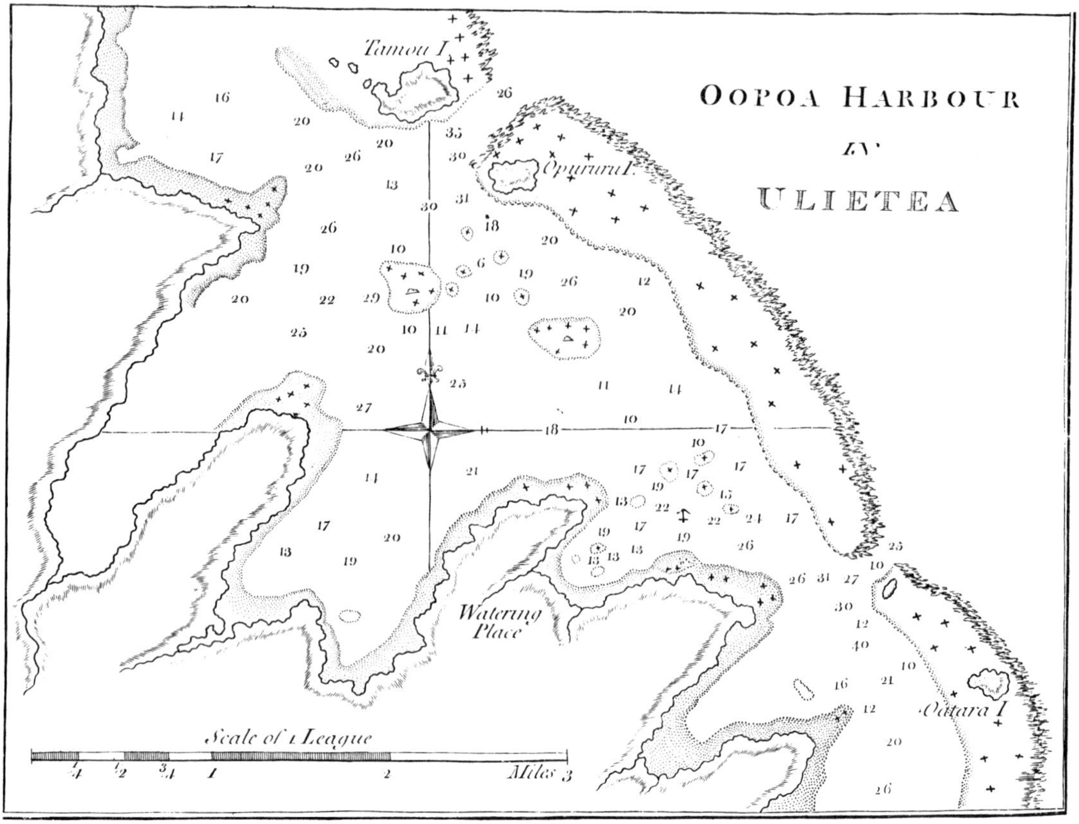

ciety Islands. It was the hereditary land of the reigning family, and the usual residence of the king and his household. But the most remarkable object connected with Opoa, was the large marae, or temple, where the national idol was worshipped, and human victims were sacrificed. These offerings were not only brought from the districts of Raiatea and the adjacent islands, but also from the windward group, and even from the more distant islands to the south and south-east.

"The worship of Oro, in the marae here, appears to have been of the most sanguinary kind; human immolation was frequent, and, in addition to the bones and other relics of the former sacrifices, now scattered among the ruins of the temple, there is still a large enclosure, the walls of which are formed entirely of human skulls. The horrid piles of skulls, in their various stages of decay, exhibit a ghastly spectacle. They are principally, if not entirely, the skulls of those who have been slain in battle. A

The Tamanu was a sacred tree of the marae, but it is widespread among the islands, especially along the shores of the lagoons. Its wood is hard with a beautiful, wavy grain. It was much prized for carving. It was also used extensively for the smaller canoes. This painting is another from Sydney Parkinson's portfolio.

number of beautiful trees grow around, especially the tamanu, *callophyllum inophyllum*, and the aoa, *ficus prolixa*, resembling, in its growth and appearance, one of the varieties of the banian in India."

Atrocities of the Areois

"These, though the general amusements of the Areois, were not the only purposes for which they assembled. They included

'All monstrous, all prodigious things;'

and these were 'abominable, unutterable.' In some of their

meetings, they appear to have placed their invention on the rack, to discover the worst pollutions of which it was possible for man to be guilty, and to have striven to outdo each other in the most revolting practices. The mysteries of iniquity, and acts of more than bestial degradation, to which they were at times addicted, must remain in the darkness in which even they felt it sometimes expedient to conceal them. I will not do violence to my own feelings, or offend those of my readers, by details of conduct, which the mind cannot contemplate without pollution and pain. I should not have alluded to them, but for the purpose of shewing the affecting debasement, and humiliating demoralization, to which ignorance, idolatry, and the evil propensities of the human heart, when uncontrolled or unrestrained by the institutions and relations of civilized society and sacred truth, are capable of reducing mankind, even under circumstances highly favourable to the culture of virtue, purity, and happiness.

"In these pastimes, in their accompanying abominations, and the often-repeated practices of the most unrelenting, murderous cruelty, these wandering Aerois passed their lives, esteemed by the people as a superior order of beings, closely allied to the gods, and deriving from them direct sanction, not only for their abominations, but even for their heartless murders. Free from labour and care, they roved from island to island, supported by the chiefs and the priests; and often feasted on plunder from the gardens of the industrious husbandman, while his own family was not unfrequently deprived thereby, for a time, of the means of subsistence. Such was their life of luxurious and licentious indolence and crime. And such was the character of their delusive system of superstition, that, for them, too, was reserved the Elysium which their fabulous mythology taught them to believe was provided, in a future state of existence, for those so preeminently favoured by the gods."

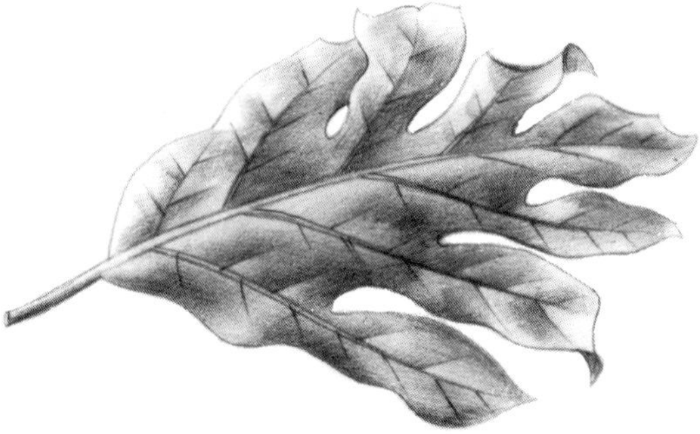

CHAPTER EIGHT

The White Man Destroyeth

More whalers and traders came in the early and middle 1800's but since their purpose was almost exclusively to replenish their stores and refresh their crews, they visited the larger island of Tahiti and for the most part passed Raiatea by. There were some callers, especially traders seeking sandalwood in the high mountains and bêche-de-mer in the lagoons, for sale in China where they were greatly prized—the first for incense and sweet-smelling carvings, the second for the pleasure these sea slugs gave to the Chinese palate. But these men of commerce left little of written interest to us . . . with one lucky exception. Frederick D. Bennett (not to be confused with the missionary of the same last name) was not a whaler. Rather, he arrived as a passenger on a whaling ship. He was a surgeon from London who wanted to see the Pacific world and in particular to study the anatomy and habits of whales. He stopped in Raiatea at 1833, some fifty years after Cook, and wrote a chapter in his book of observations which is, in my opinion, the best account of life on our island during the days before the French conquest. It was then, and perhaps always had been, enough apart from Tahiti to preserve a distinct individuality of its own. Indeed Bennett's account makes me think nostalgically of my own first visit nearly a hundred years later and it even sounds some echoes of Raiatea today. Though he repeats much that has gone before, I would like to quote him at length because he writes so well and because he is so sensitive, especially to the physical loveliness of the island. Let us call it recapitulation, or perhaps farewell to old-time Raiatea:

"Upon approaching Raiatea and passing through the eastern aperture in the reef which encircles its coast, a

A view of Uturoa from D'Urville's *Voyages au Tour du Monde.* Judging by the turbulence of the waters in the foreground, the scene is depicted from the pass where Surgeon Bennett came through the "narrow and dangerous channel." Actually it is one of the easiest and safest reef passes in the islands. Huge cruise ships nowadays negotiate it easily.

scene of great beauty was unfolded to our view: the lofty and well-vegetated mountains of the interior of the land arose before us in sombre majesty, and at less than a stone's-throw on either side of our route a coral islet, covered with vegetation, and set as an emerald in the bosom of the lagoon water, communicated a refreshing odour to the serene morning air; the whole offering charms which scarcely permitted us to notice the narrow and dangerous channel we were threading, with a raging surf beating violently upon the reef within a short distance on either side of the ship. A few minutes sufficed to carry us through this passage, when we experienced a sudden transition from the sea in its most raging and destructive form, to the same water under its most isolated and reposing aspect.

"As we glided slowly along the coast, groups of natives assembled on the beach, gazing at our approach, and welcoming, with their wild cries, the arrival of a ship to whose almost annual visits they had been for many years accustomed; and we had scarcely cast anchor in the harbour of Utumaoro before the decks were crowded with the same people, attired in holyday costume, their heads adorned with chaplets of wild flowers, or green and fragrant leaves, and all bearing in their hands baskets of fruit and shells, either for barter, or as presents for their European friends.

"Though limited in its extent, Raiatea has a bold and mountainous appearance, and is no less picturesque than

This "cascade" forms a delicious swimming pool tucked in the steep valley behind the great vertical rock at Haapapara.

Tahiti. A dense garment of foliage clothes its surface, from the vallies to the mountain heights; and although occasional naked cliffs, and crags of black rock, start from the verdure to arrest the eye by their powerful relief, they can scarcely be said to intrude unpleasantly upon the general air of unbounded fertility that pervades the soil.

"The extent of perfectly level land is not great, and seldom extends farther than a few hundred yards from the sea-shore, but some broad and fertile vallies rise from the coast to the interior with a gentle acclivity, and deep and gloomy ravines occupy the intervals between the abrupt faces of the mountains. The entire island is but too well watered, mountain-streams, cascades, and swamps, abounding in every direction. The soil is exceedingly fertile, and repays generously the slightest labour bestowed on its cultivation.

One of my favorite spots that "arrest the eye" is this little pinnacle that peeps between these two high peaks above Avera as you sail down the lagoon from Uturoa on the way to Fetuna.

"Few natural objects are so well calculated to excite wonder in the human mind as the coral constructions, in all their Protean forms, that surround the greater number of Polynesian islands, and which demonstrate so perfectly the power of nature to effect her vast designs through apparently feeble and inefficient agents. It requires, indeed, an intimate acquaintance with the habits of the lithophites, and ocular proof of their labours, to credit what stupendous submarine reefs, and islands many miles in compass, are indebted for at least their entire visible structure, to the secretory economy of these tiny architects.

"In such examples Raiatea is not deficient. On the contrary, she is indebted for a large share of her natural beauties, as well as commercial advantages, to the coral fabrics which surround her shores. These chiefly obtain in the form of reefs; of which the nature and use may be best understood by considering them under their natural divisions of a *barrier-* and a *shore-reef*. The former encircles the island, as a breakwater or sea-wall, at the distance of one and a half or two miles from the land; presenting a precipitous face to the ocean, to receive the assault of its billows, but encroaching in a superficial and capricious manner upon the lagoon water it encloses. The shore-reef is continuous with the land around the entire coast, and stretches into the sea to a variable, but usually to a very considerable, distance. Its greater portion is covered with shallow water, which in many parts does not exceed, and is often less than a foot in depth; its outer margin shelves irregularly, and terminates abruptly in a deep channel of blue water. This channel (which is also continued round the island) furnishes a natural division between the two principal reefs, as well as a convenient passage for navigation. Coral islets, shoals, or whatever other form the madreporic rock may assume, can be distinctly traced to one or the other of these apparently distinct reefs, but never occur as the productions of both conjointly.

"The outer or *barrier-reef* resembles a wall no less in its structure than in its office: unlike the friable and arborescent material we commonly associate with the name of coral, the rock of which it is composed is hard, compact, and amorphous, bearing much resemblance to a very firm cement; and it is only on its shoals, extending towards the land, that we notice the elegant form of the tree-coral, contrasting so strongly with the rocky and unornamental structure on which it is planted, as to justify a doubt if both are constructed by the same animals. The summit of this reef is flat; several yards in breadth; but little raised above the level of the sea; and washed by a heavy surf, which breaks against its sea-aspect, courses over its level surface, and falls gently, and as it were by a line of cascades, into the placid basin on the opposite side. At ebb tide, when the surf is less in amount, this reef is partly dry and accessible; but when the tide is high, or the weather tempestuous, the sea, raised into lofty and magnificent arches, beats over the rocky barrier with terrific grandeur, and with a rolling or thundering sound which may be heard, on a tranquil night, at the distance of several miles. To persons unaccustomed to such scenes, nothing is more deeply and agreeably impressive than the view of a majestic surf thus lashing the coast of an island opposed to the play of a mighty ocean.

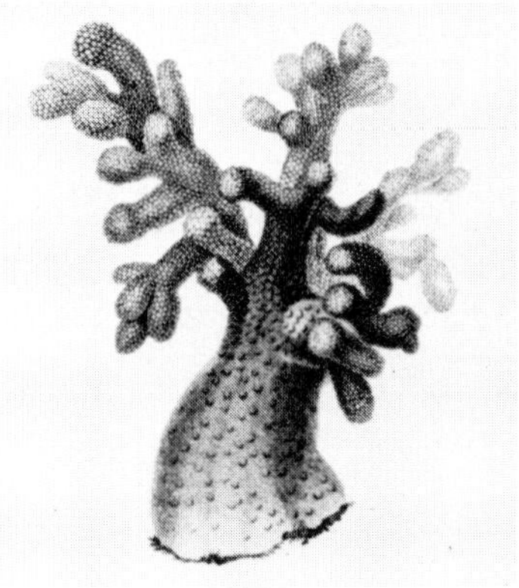

"The *shore-reef* is chiefly composed of amorphous rock, or block-coral; though tree-coral is also abundant upon it, as well as extensive beds of sand. In many parts, where the water is deep, it presents a submarine picture of extreme beauty: extensive coral groves, planted in beds of smooth and white sand, and mingling hues of pink, blue, white, and yellow, appear through the transparent sea; numerous small fish, of brilliant colours, glide over the sands, thread the labyrinths of the coral branches, or, when alarmed, dart rapidly for shelter into the recesses of the stony thickets; the whole affording a peculiarly pleasing, and almost kaleidescopic effect.

"There is, however, no feature in the scenery of this coast that strikes the European observer as more novel and lovely than the verdant islets, or motus, which strew the expanse of smooth sea between the barrier reef and the main land. They are composed entirely of coral; are raised scarcely three feet above the level of the surrounding water; and appear to be peculiar to the barrier reef. They are most usually based upon the shoals which con-

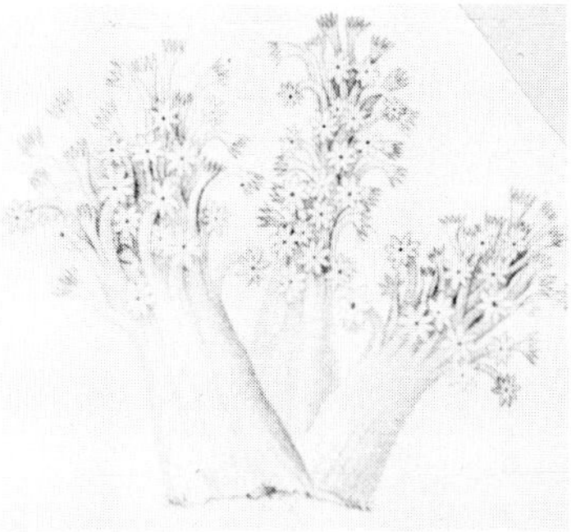

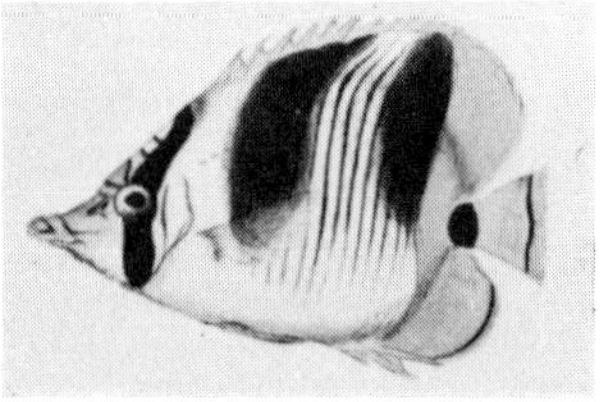

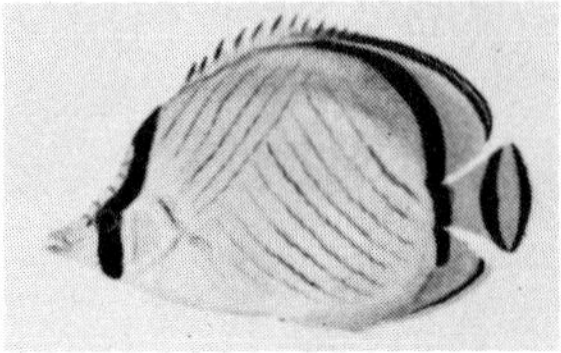

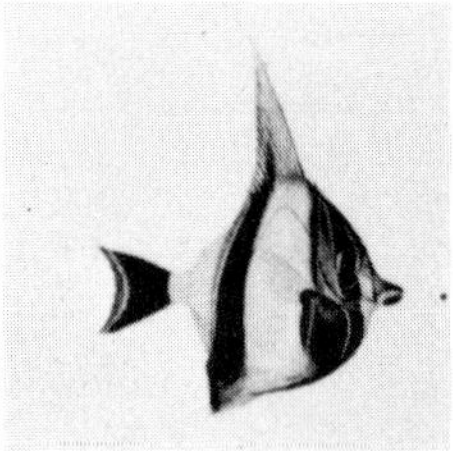

stitute the lateral boundaries of the reef apertures. It is probable that they are formed from mature coral shoals, which, after they had been raised to the surface of the sea, had caused the water to recede from their centre by the increase and elevation of their circumference—the near approach to a circular form they invariably present being in favour of this supposition.

"A tide of some power runs through the channel between the great reef and the shore. Its rise and fall is inconsiderable, (seldom exceeding a few inches,) but its changes occur with remarkable regularity; the water being invariably highest at noon and midnight, and lowest at six in the morning and at the same hour in the evening.*

"The whole island is arbitrarily divided into districts and spots; to each of which the natives give an appropriate name, however small, barren, or inaccessible the tract

* He is referring to the sun tides, a phenomenon peculiar to these islands. (Author's note)

may be.* Cultivated lands are not numerous, and are chiefly planted with sweet-potatoes, sugar-cane, or arrow-root. The natives' dwellings are constructed with a primitive simplicity which speaks more in favour of the serenity of the climate than of the domestic disposition of the occupants. Their interior contains sleeping mats spread on the floor, and provided with small pillows filled with cotton; (which have greatly superseded, but not altogether exploded, the use of the tuaurau, or ancient wooden pillow); low wooden stools, nohoraa, in the ancient fashion; an umete and penu, or trough and stone pestle, used in preparing their favourite vegetable paste the poe; scraped cocoa nut shells, used as cups; a mallet and plank for the manufacture of bark cloth; a fishing spear or net; and a musket. Bunches of edible fruits are suspended from the walls; and occasionally a matronly sow, with a numerous litter, occupies a corner of the common apartment fenced

* Both the Georgian and Society Islanders have a strong prejudice against selling any portion of their lands. They have no precedent, they say, for such a practice, and are unwilling to commence it; consequently, no instance has yet occurred of foreigners obtaining land at any of these islands, on other terms than by the purchase of a long lease, or by a grant, which the government can at any time retract.

These pictures of the inside and outside of old-time houses were taken by Kenneth Emory in the twenties and are in the Bishop Museum files. Although a hundred years later than Surgeon Bennett, they are probably a fair representation of the living quarters which the missionaries were tearing down so that the Raiateans could live in European-type houses "more comfortable than they wished to be." The house on the water is at Opoa, also in the 1920's and it does not take much imagination to envision its owner sitting in the doorway with his fishing pole. He might be there today.

off for her accommodation. A separate shed is employed for cooking; and a plot of enclosed land, planted with useful vegetables or favourite flowers, surrounds many of the huts. Some dwellings with boarded floors, and supported on piles, are erected over the shallow waters of the shore-reef at some distance from the land. The native, residing in this eccentric situation, may be often seen seated on his haunches fishing with rod and line from the threshold of his door, and tossing the small fry he captures upon the embers of a fire within, where his wife attends to their cooking.

"Strenuous exertions have been made by well intentioned missionaries to prevail upon these islanders to construct their habitations in the neat and substantial style of English cottages, and to substitute ornamental towns for groups of huts. Laws were framed for this purpose; and the recusants had their old fashioned tenements destroyed over their heads, that they might have every incentive to commence the new and improved system. The plan was attended with no useful or permanent result; the people soon wearied in the labour of erecting more complicated buildings, while their simple huts answered every desir-

able purpose, and have now reverted to their former abodes; leaving some ruinous wattled and plastered cottages, as mementos of the attempt to make them more comfortable than they wished to be.

"The number of inhabitants this island contains does not exceed 1700,* though the soil, if properly applied, is capable of maintaining a population of more than treble that amount. In personal appearance the natives are not to be distinguished from Tahitians. They are a well-formed race, in average stature superior to Europeans, and their frames proportionately muscular. They have all that plumpness and smoothness of skin peculiar to Asiatics who enjoy a comfortable mode of life; but corpulence is comparatively rare amongst them, and by no means peculiar to the chiefs, who are often slender, while some of the inferior people are extremely stout. The clear brown complexion they possess is many shades darker in some individuals than in others, and in a few instances

* The English mission's estimate in 1834 was also 1700. The French administration estimated 2135 in 1897 but perhaps the 500 prisoners of war expatriated in that year should be added. The current population circa 1970 is probably about 4000.

Here is a random selection of Polynesian faces of today from our own immediate neighborhood in Fetuna. From left to right they are: the young wife of one of our local schoolteachers; one of Narii's several brothers; Ro'o, the master catcher of turtles, and his wife.

almost amounts to blackness, without any apparent cause (as extraordinary exposure to the sun) to account for the difference. Their hair, also, which is generally black and glossy, assumes in a few instances a light or reddish colour in the adults and a flaxen hue in the children. Their features are pleasing, occasionally handsome, and express much contentment and good humour; in some individuals (perhaps more particularly among the higher ranks) they present a regularity of outline, a thinness of the lips, and a prominence of nose (approaching to the aquiline) which brings them nearer to the European cast. A flat or perpendicular occiput is very remarkable in the heads of this people, and, as well as a confluent nose, is esteemed a trait of beauty. Both these valued peculiarities are therefore encouraged in childhood; the former, the nurse endeavours to improve, by supporting the infant only by the feet and the back of the head; and the latter, by occasionally retouching the original model of the nose by firm pressure with the palm of the hand.

"The women of Raiatea are, for the most part, disproportionately shorter than the men. The pleasing expression, rather than the regularity of their features, entitles many of them to be termed pretty, if not handsome. Their eyes are sparkling and expressive; their teeth are conspicuous for size, regularity, and whiteness; and their smile is peculiarly captivating. I have looked in vain, however, for the grace, or elegance of figure, so much praised in these, and other Polynesian females: although well proportioned, their figures are too developed and masculine to be graceful. They stand awkwardly, with their feet set widely apart, and their toes turned in almost to deformity; while their general carriage is careless, and indicative of the crouching sedentary posture in which they commonly indulge.

"Neither sex is remarkable for an agreeable voice; and although the dialect they employ is melodious, and capable of much softness in pronunciation, their mode of speaking it is clamorous and discordant.

"It is difficult to define the disposition of this people, since its most prominent feature is caprice. They are, however, shrewd and intelligent observers; strongly disposed to mirth; mild and peaceable unless excited by any act of injustice; and familiar and hospitable towards foreigners. They are naturally indolent, but are capable of bearing a fair proportion of labour, and when trained to the habits of Europeans are not deficient in mental or physical power.* They are certainly covetous; but the feeling assumes in them that childish and inconsistent character that leads them to obtain some desired property, which, its value diminishing with possession, is soon after as freely bestowed as it was anxiously acquired. In their conduct toward each other they are generous; and no reproach is so hurtful to their feelings as that of avarice. Vanity, with its concomitant, the dread of ridicule and censure, is a prominent feature in their character: we were often amused by observing the tact with which one native would play upon this weak point in another, and by dint of flattery obtain the grant of some desired favour.

"They betray much inclination to indulge in false statements; though the latter are usually of the character which some moralists have bleached, as being unattended by the wish or power to injure. This habit chiefly prevails with the young ladies who sit down to a *paraparou* or gossiping party, and, who, when their stock of facts is exhausted, amuse each other with many tales of their own invention. Should any foreigner be present, and remark upon the falsity of their statements, they express neither surprise nor confusion, but coolly reply, "was it not so?—you know best—perhaps it was not so;" but should any one of the gossips take the same liberty, the narrator bridles up with an indignant look, and vents a petulant expression that defies orthography, but which is highly expressive of disgust at the ill-manners of her companion.

"Their language has no word beyond *maitai*, good, to

* A Society Islander can, upon an emergency, undergo much more fatigue than an European; and although, during an ordinary journey, he will often sit down to rest when his white companion thinks such relaxation unnecessary, this indolence arises rather from a habit he has contracted of making himself comfortable than from any inability to endure exertion.

acknowledge the receipt of a kindness; nor has it any equivalent to "gratitude;" and there is reason to believe that the feeling itself is *rather* more deficient in these people than in Europeans.

"Neither sex is at all social in domestic life. The treatment of the women is now in no way objectionable: the wife shares with the husband the duties of their station, the more laborious being assigned to the man. The majority of the married women have a potential voice in domestic arrangements, and in traffic it is often difficult to get a man to conclude a bargain until his wife has been consulted. The removal of some ancient prejudices has raised the native woman to her proper grade in society; but while her physical condition is thus improved, the same advance is not perceptible in her moral character. Chas-

Gauguin's title for this painting is "Ta Matete." "The Market place," but it might just as well have been Parauparau, which means literally "Talk, Talk," but which is a favorite expression in the islands for the endless gossipy conversations, male or female or both, that the Polynesians love. Although it, in turn, is three generations later than Bennett, it fits comfortably into context and might by him have been entitled "Was It Not So?" Moreover, today, three more generations after Gauguin, it is still an instantly familiar scene. The Polynesians do not change much. Long may they continue so.

Two more Fetuna faces, Turo's paternal and his adoptive grandmothers. Perhaps they are deploring the licentiousness of their offspring, but I doubt it. Indeed they may well be recollecting nostalgically the good times of their own girlhoods.

tity is not esteemed a virtue either in the single or married state; on the contrary, licentiousness is so interwoven with the national habits that a virtuous female is here a rare exception to her sex, is held in no esteem, and is seldom to be met with even in name—a remark which does not except the blood royal, nor even the most devout members of the church. The missionaries have been naturally anxious to suppress so prominent a vice; but in no part of their task have they been less successful. The strict laws enacted on this subject have tended but to restrain the more open profligacy; and unless delinquents can be made liable to the same moral punishments as in well ordered nations, no radical amendment can be expected.

"When travelling over this island we found the natives active and trustworthy guides. The care they displayed in pointing out the most practicable paths over the rugged hills, in conducting, unasked, to the limpid streams in the vicinity of our route, climbing for cocoa nuts, or offering the wild sugar cane they had gathered in the thickets, and, above all, a practice they have, when passing through dense brushwood, of breaking the elastic boughs they displace, that they might not recoil upon their companions following in their trail, were attentions it was impossible not to appreciate. There is, perhaps, no situation in which a Raiatean appears to greater advantage than when thus performing the office of a guide through his native wilds.

"The very young stipe of the cocoa-nut palm affords the females one of the most delicate and beautiful ornaments they possess: when peeled into long strips and dried, it is thin, transparent, pure white, and glossy, and when worn as rosettes in the hair, bears a close similitude to white satin ribbon. The dried leaves of the Pandanus, or the long culms of a grass, named *nanimu*, fastened together in long and slender bundles, are the materials chiefly used in manufacturing the hats worn by the men.

"The ancient practice of tatooing the skin is gradually declining amongst the Society Islanders generally. The missionaries have been much opposed to the custom, and

If you were walking up the "limped stream" that flows from the cascade at Haapapara, your considerate guide would part the purau branches so that you could have a look at these ancient petroglyphs of the turtle and the shark, familiar and evidently revered symbols, but symbols of what? The significance of the many petroglyphs scattered all over the islands is lost in the past. The Raiateans will tell you that they were carved before their forefathers came here and no one knows why.

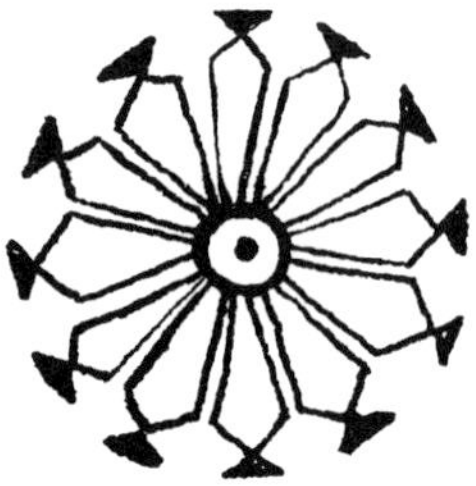

among the laws framed for these islands was one which made tatooing criminal; but this has been since repealed, or continues in force only in the islands of Huahine, Raiatea, and Tahaa.

"The older natives of both sexes are very handsomely and profusely tatooed from the waist to the toes; the back of the hand and fingers are similarly adorned; but the face is either untouched, or marked with only a few punctures. But few of the natives excel in the art of tatooing. Those who are deformed with hump-backs bear the greatest share of reputation amongst their countrymen; probably from the circumstance of their devoting themselves more exclusively to this less laborious employment.

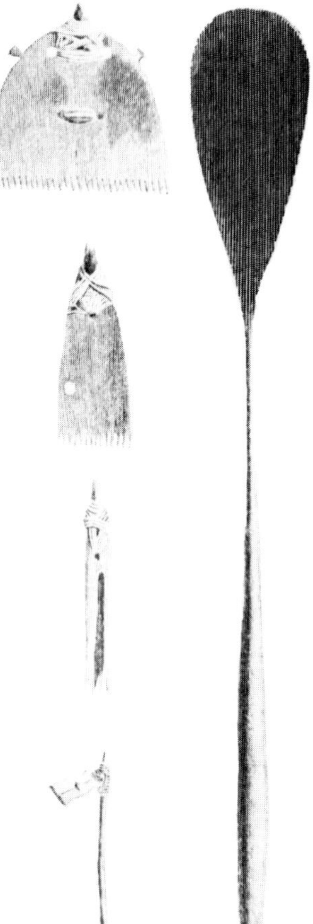

"While at this island, I gratified a wish to observe the process and effects of the tatoo by having a figure thus impressed upon myself. The artist I engaged was a Tahitian; and from the numerous patterns displayed on his person we selected a circular figure, named *pote*; the spot I preferred devoting to the impression was the upper arm. The operation commenced by bending the elastic rib of a cocoa-nut leaf into a circular form, and smearing its edge with a black fluid composed of the lamp black of burned candle-nuts diluted to the consistence of printers' ink. This placed on the skin marked the outer circle; to execute which by the eye alone would have proved a difficult task; the remainder of the design, however, was completed without any similar guide. The tatooing instrument, (a thin plate of boar's tusk, about half an inch in breadth, sharply toothed at its margin, and fixed, at an angle, to the extremity of a slender handle), was then imbued with the black fluid, and made to penetrate the skin by striking short and quick strokes on its handle with a second and heavier piece of wood, of conical form; the artist desisting after every few taps, to wipe away the ink and oozing blood, that he might observe better the effect produced and the line to follow. In less than an hour the design was completed. The pain produced by the operation was rather annoying than severe. It was only felt during the application of the toothed instrument, when the sensation was of a dull pricking nature, hard to endure when long protracted and felt much more sensitively in some parts of the skin than in others. The bleeding from the punctures was trifling at first; but as the work proceeded, and the stimulus determined the blood more freely to the surface, each application of the instrument was attended with a greater flow. The arm continued inflamed, and a red serum oozed from the punctures for several hours; but on the following day the part was merely tender, and the redness of the skin had given place to a bruised appearance, (from extravasated blood,) extending to the elbow, (an effect of course not perceptible in the dark skin of the native;) while the effused serum gave the tatooed figure a varnished appearance. In four days the arm was perfectly well; and the scarf skin peeling off, left the tatooed marks beneath of a bright-blue colour and slightly elevated.

"Bread-fruit, mountain-plantains, bananas, cocoa-nuts, and South Sea chestnuts, spontaneously produced on the soil, form the daily food of these islanders. Sweet potatoes, taro-roots, and yams, are less generally used, in proportion to the labour requisite for their cultivation. Hogs and domestic fowls, though numerous, are rarely consumed by their owners, who prefer reserving them for traffic with foreign shipping. Fish is much valued; but as the larger and better kinds are rare on the coast and troublesome to obtain, the natives commonly substitute, as an addition to their vegetable diet, the small fishes, crabs, and shell-fish, they daily procure on the reefs. They eat the soft parts of the *emehama*, when the ocean throws that mollusc within their reach; and the large sea-urchin, they esteem a good food, vast quantities of its shells and spines, piled on different parts of the sea shore, denoting where the people have enjoyed a feast of this kind. They cook in the ancient mode. When a large bulk of food is to be dressed, a deep excavation in the ground is lined with stones and filled with ignited fuel; the pit being sufficiently heated, the embers are removed, and the stones swept clean, and covered with leaves, on which the provisions are laid; the whole is then covered over with leaves, heated stones and earth. An entire hog, of any required size, its abdomen filled with leaves and heated stones, is thus thoroughly and quickly cooked. Its skin is

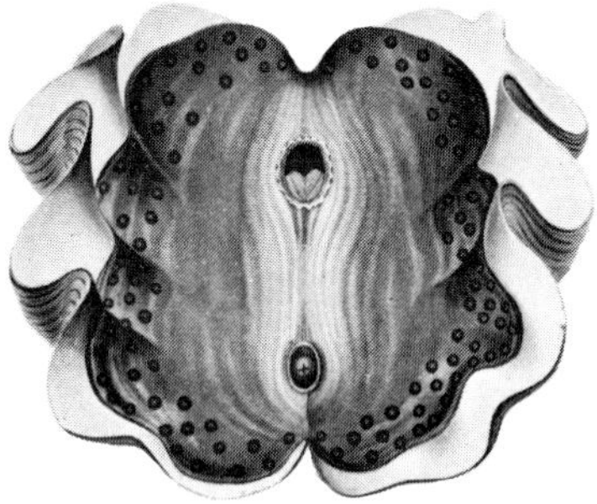

Another of Dr. Emory's early photographs taken from Tahaa.

not changed in colour, the animal juices are well retained, and the flavour of the meat is excellent. The term baking is not strictly descriptive of this process, which is one intermediate to baking and cooking by steam. In preparing a family meal, the provisions are cooked in a more summary manner by roasting them over a surface of stones and ignited fuel, placed in a shallow circular excavation in the earth, and resembling a small lime-kiln.

"The vegetable paste, or *poe*, so peculiar to the diet of Polynesian nations, is here prepared either from the bread-fruit or mountain-plantain; the cooked fruit being put into a trough, and beaten with a stone pestle to the state of a uniform and plastic pulp. The *poe fei*, or mountain-plantain *poe*, is the pride of the natives, and is almost peculiar to this island and Tahiti. From the arrow-root, or *pia*, combined with the pulp of young cocoa-nuts, they prepare small compact puddings, of rich but agreeable taste. They also prepare some good jellies from the same flour, mingled with bananas or other native fruits, and cooked in bamboos.

"With their animal food the Raiateans employ sea-water as a substitute for salt; each morsel of flesh being dipped in a cocoa-nut shell of that fluid placed by their side at the

meal. As a condiment to the bread-fruit they use *mitiaro*, or grated cocoa-nut kernels, sprinkled with salt water and carefully fermented. It possesses a rich and sharp taste, which may be compared to that of cheese. The latter European food, however, is compared by the natives to their fermented bread-fruit, and named by them *teoo papa*, or white man's *teoo*.

"The pure element from the mountain stream, or the fluid contained in the young cocoa-nut, is the more usual beverage of these islanders; though many of them will indulge to excess in the ardent spirits which they obtain by barter from foreign vessels—a traffic much to be deprecated, and one in which it is to be hoped no master of a ship would engage, unless compelled by the sternest necessity.* They procure, also, from the neighbouring is-

This still much older wash drawing by Sydney Parkinson, executed on Cook's first visit in 1769, when he "discovered" Raiatea, is entitled "View between Ulietea & Otaha." The views seem strikingly alike and show perhaps that the scenery had not changed much more than the people. Today, however, if my orientation is correct, you would see an airstrip across the water

* I feel reluctant to attach blame to the shipping of the United States of America, lest it should be construed into the pettiness of national prejudice; but it would, on the other hand, be unjust to conceal the fact, that the "temperate ships," so numerously sent forth from American ports, are actually the principal purveyors of ardent spirits to the natives of these islands. Their crews, (themselves conscientiously abstaining from spirits,) are usually provided with a large quantity of rum, for the sole purpose of conducting a lucrative traffic with the Polynesians; while the latter are but too eager to make sacrifices to obtain this inviting but pernicious luxury.

Piper inebrians.

land of Borabora a large quantity of a colourless liquor distilled from the bread-fruit. This spirit is sufficiently strong, and bears some resemblance to whisky. The natives name it *ava*,* after the intoxicating drink they formerly prepared from the roots of the *Piper methisticum*, the use of which is now obsolete, and the plant itself almost extinct on these islands.

"The systematic manner in which the natives intoxicate themselves is not the least curious feature in their character. They will refrain long from spirits, or very abruptly relinquish their use, but when inclined to indulge, nothing short of the most complete inebriety will satisfy them. Many amongst them consider that a moderate use of ardent spirits is tantalizing and disagreeable, and will often refuse to partake of any, unless they can obtain enough to produce the "happiest" effects. During our present visit to Raiatea the vice of intoxication was not so prevalent as we found it at a subsequent period; yet, on every fresh importation of liquor from Borabora, it was common to see the more debauched islanders parading the settlement in a state of riotous intoxication, linked arm-in-arm for mutual support, and with bottles of spirits slung round their bodies and cocoa-nut shells in their hands, occasionally pausing to drink, then renewing their route, yelling like demons, until, incapable of further advance, they expended their last gleam of reason in seeking the nearest shed for a swinish repose.

"The labours of the missionaries are in no way rendered so nugatory as by the abuse of spirits amongst the natives; while it is equally evident, that unless effective, and above all permanent, measures are not adopted to check this increasing evil, the extermination of the aboriginal tribes will be as rapid as inevitable."

* A second, and more figurative name, occasionally applied to this liquor, is *pape pepe*, or the water that flogs.

Opposite
Sydney Parkinson has left us a lovely piece of pictorial evidence of the "obsolete" *Piper methisticum,* Ava, although it was the root, not the leaf or stem, which provided the mild narcotic drink that was such a favorite in the olden days before our alcohol routed it. Dare we compare our missionaries' routing their religion? Kava is still a great favorite in the islands of the Raiatean's ancestors, Tonga, Samoa, and Fiji.

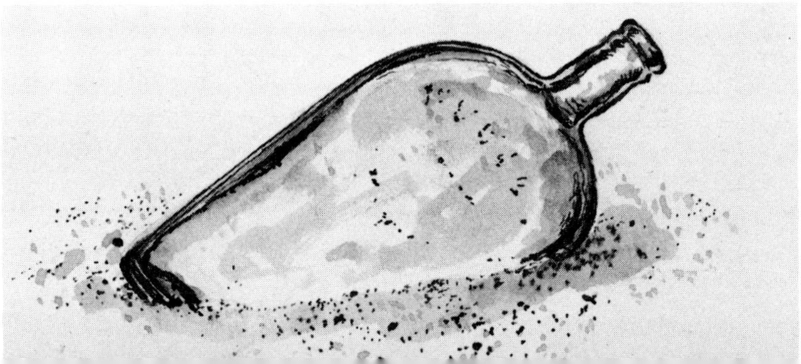

CHAPTER NINE

Farewell

After the period recounted in this first-hand report on old-time Raiatea, nostalgically re-echoing the prehistoric past (in spite of its recent blemishes of contact), comes the sad story of the French conquest. The usual preliminary pattern of the world's surrender to Europe was now being repeated: 1) the discoverers had found the "new" land, 2) the missionaries had gone forth to convert and had often been driven out, sometimes tortured and killed, 3) now it was time for the navies and armies (agents, one might say, of their backers, the merchants) to avenge righteously the atrocities inflicted on the men of the Gospel and, incidentally of course, to take over the rule of the "primitive" peoples and the "new" land, for their own purposes.

In our islands, soon after surgeon Bennett's visit, this process commenced in Tahiti. For some decades there had been doubts whether that jewel of the Pacific would go to the English or the French. England had prior claim, by right of discovery, and a discovery in those days—by a first hoisting of the flag and a reading of a proclamation, later confirmed by official publication, was conceded to be internationally binding. But, of course, the virtue of discovery would fade without military and commercial follow-through, and, having driven the French from America and having discovered New Zealand, and, thanks to Cook, Australia, the British lion had apparently assembled for his feast about all the prey he could digest. With such vast, potentially rich domains to exploit in the Pacific, why should England bother with a scattering of far-distant islands? Although the frightened Tahitians sought an affiliation with the English, Queen Victoria was cool to Queen Pomare's overtures. It was only natural that the

French, thwarted elsewhere (though not by any means everywhere), should step in, and Tahiti was brought under their guns by Admiral Du Petit-Thouars in 1842. His coup de force was subsequently ratified by Louis Philipe, and the Tricolor was raised over the island in 1843. It still flies there, though of late it has seemed to quaver a bit.

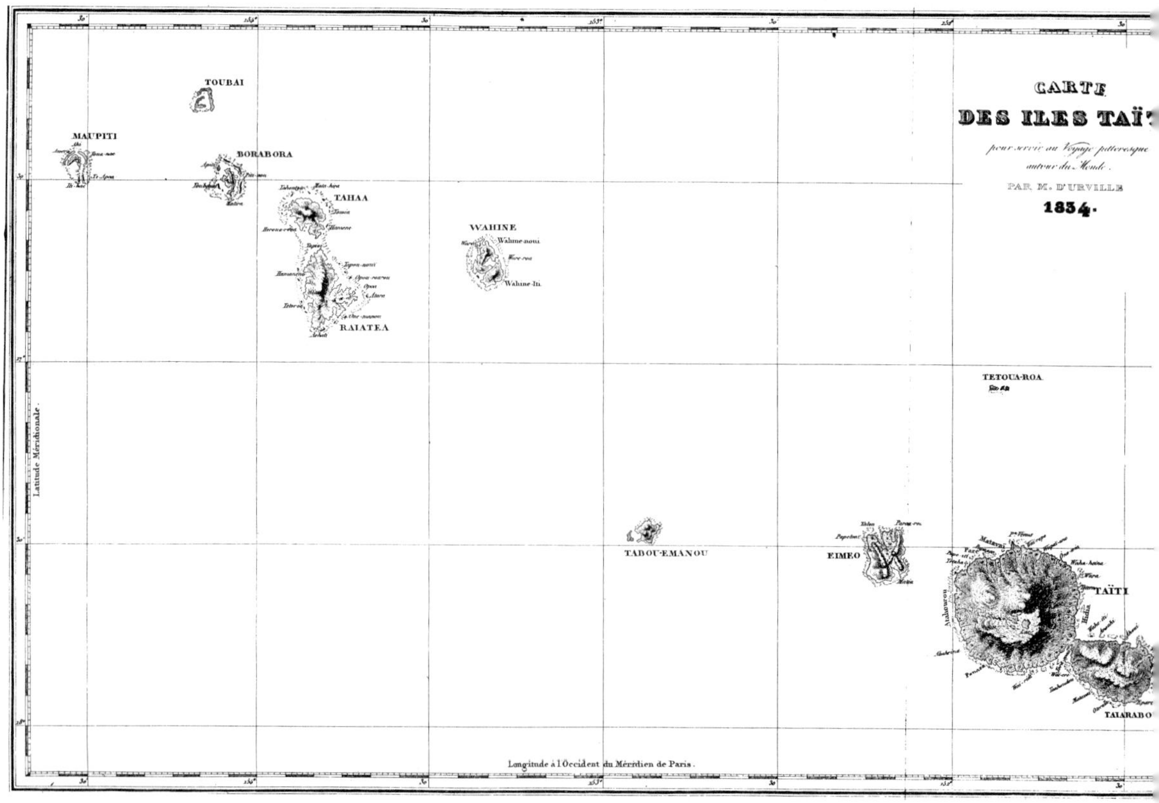

But Raiatea? There the proud Tamatoa asserted their independence and, as of old, the superiority of the sacred red girdle (in spirit if not in actual feathers). They recognized the inevitability of European sovereignty, but they opted for the Union Jack rather than the Tricolor. After all why should a Tamatoa follow the surrender of a Pomare? Attempts at subjugation were made by the French for a short time; then there occurred a curious interlude, beginning in 1847, when France agreed that the leeward islands (Raiatea, Tahaa, Huahine, Bora Bora, and Maupiti) would fall to the lot of the English. But that treaty was broken in 1888. Perhaps because our island was not a rich military or commercial prize, or perhaps, as I prefer to think, because its people were such fierce, determined fighters, a large-scale assault upon it was conveniently postponed. There were other factors. Long before its "discovery" by Europeans, Tahiti had been divided into at least three large, clan-ruled sections and many more semi-independent chiefdoms. It was not difficult for the newly arrived intruder to set district against district, to divide and conquer. Raiatea was united. The Tamatoa were supreme. They had suffered local defeats at times from Bora Bora, but these set-backs seemed always to have been absorbed, by marriage, by treaty, by default. So the island stood as one.

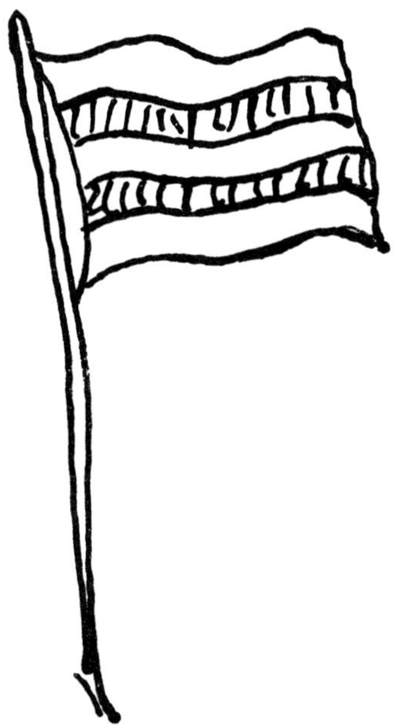

Each of the Leeward Islands had its own flag in those days. Raiatea's was two red stripes and three white ones.

Raiatea's geography too made it unappetizing to European naval and marine action. Its defenders could retreat up into their narrow valleys and, with surprize raids, could bleed the invaders on the narrow shores. The Raiateans were old hands at this game, having had much experience over the centuries with the Pora Pora warriors of the silent paddle. The white man was a new hand at the game, and he had not much stomach for such punishment, either in anticipation or in actuality.

But when the French imposed an import tariff in Tahiti in 1892, English and American businessmen began using Raiatea as a free port, and could thus undercut French merchants in the islands. The situation became intolerable and at last French national pride and a desire to gather all the islands together led them to a major effort. In 1897, more than fifty years or two generations after the conquest of Tahiti, two ships of war arrived under the command of Gustave Gallet, the arrogant and imperious minister who had been the arch enemy of Paul Gauguin. The marines mounted a full-scale attack, with massive firepower, driving the Raiateans back, valley by valley, until at last Teraupoo, the surrogate chief, was captured and exiled to New Caledonia. Five hundred prisoners were dispatched to the Marquesas, and at last resistance collapsed. The prisoners were repatriated in a couple of years, and the flag of France flew over Raiatea in 1898.

The currently reigning Tamatoa, however, never collapsed. In a characteristically Polynesian way, he had turned over to a lower-born delegate the privilege of surrender. He held himself aloof and, as we may imagine, vanished with the sacred red girdle reserved for himself and his descendants forever.

This last is, of course, a fanciful interpretation which cannot be buttressed by actual evidence. But it is a Polynesian kind of interpretation, and my guess is that when the French are forced to leave, as I am convinced they will be some day, just as they and their fellow Europeans have been all over the world; my fond speculation is that a future Tamatoa will return from the lofty heights of the tapu twin mountains above Opoa, that he will recite his ancient geneology, that he will be recognized by his people, even after long subjugation and exile, that he will then wrap the red girdle about his loins and stand tall once more before the great coronation stone at Taputapuatea. Whether this is all a bemused dream or not, of one thing we can be tolerably sure: the lofty stone, Tepapaoruea, and the marae will still be there.

And so at last our proud little island lost its ancient mana. It may not have been the first time in its long, long history. There may have been many shifts of power and glory in the dim Polynesian past. Certainly there had been a religious revolution when the cult of Oro came; another one when the cult of Christ arrived. A physical revolution had taken place when the white man's diseases all but wiped out the population. The French conquest was an inevitable revolution of firearms and force. And still to come was the technological revolution of compulsory

French schooling; of radios, outboards, motor scooters; and last and perhaps most frightening of all, of tourists. You might think this all a tragic ending to a lovely dream, but there is a phoenix-like power of regeneration in our little island. It has had magic enough over the past fifty-odd years to hold me under its age-old spell. But my idyll, too, seems to have reached an end. I told you early it was a love affair, nothing but a love affair, and like all love affairs, it must now have a sorrowful ending.

Camille and I have been living in our Fetuna house, roughly every other year, for two or three or four months at a time, over a dozen or so years. It has been good living, because it has been as isolated as it was fifty years ago when I first came there. No electricity, no road (and thus no autos or scooters), plenty of water, sweet from the mountains. We have built our own little wharf, reaching out in the lagoon to le bleu, where the coral plunges and the snorkelling is the best in the world. But now our spell is over. Turo and Farika have seven children (five girls and—at last!—a boy and, then, another girl). Indeed, they may have several more by the time this is in print. We don't feel we can move them out any longer, even to as copious and always hospitable house as Narii's. Moreover, the road has now been built down the west coast from Uturoa, and our house sits only a few yards between the busses and the lagoon. Moreover again, the islet of Nao Nao has been bought by a developer in Tahiti, who is selling it off in lots to vacationists and tourists, so our serene le bleu will soon be crisscrossed by water skiers. There will be electricity and in time, no doubt, a hotel.

All this presents a lively prospect for Turo, for he is by nature a manager par excellence, and he plans to open a bar. Most importantly, it will mean that he can make enough money to live on in Fetuna with his family. (The alternative he and almost all natives of these islands have been facing for many years is a long spell of identured labor in New Caledonia, where the economy is booming and workers are scarce.) Economically the central Polynesian islands are in a hapless state. Copra is almost valueless, because of chemical competitors. Vanilla flavoring comes much more cheaply from the laboratory than from

the steep tropical hills. Bananas are too far from markets, beef is restricted on such rugged, rocky lands. So, there is nothing left at home but tourists. They inevitably congregate in thick, guided streams, beating their identical paths from cruise ships or charter flights to hotels, feasts, and trinket shops and back again. If you are Polynesian you have to live in Tahiti or near the scattered hotel compounds to service them, and even then living is scant because of competition. Well, perhaps enough of the more adventurous tourists and French residents of Tahiti will come to Fetuna to keep Turo and his family busy and well fed. We hope they will, but we shan't go back again . . . at least not for more than a few days' visit, at times, to freshen the corners of our past. We have been fortunate. We are without regrets. We never could have hoped for more or for better. The erstwhile Fetunas of the earth are fast disappearing, and we must make no moans.

So we sigh philosophically and bid farewell to the golden past. But there lurks a fugitive, though stubborn suspicion that a grandchild of mine, be he or she of blood or of spirit, may one day climb the ancient Temehani and look about with wonder at the flowers in his midst, look down to the little green motus dotting the churning reef of the purple lagoon below, and look up to the stately Trade Wind clouds marching majestically under the blazing blue sky, over the deep and dark blue ocean.

Ia orana outou i te atua!

Appendix

1. The Glottal Stop and Other Polynesian Idiosyncrasies

The Polynesians in the central Pacific (and some other groups as well) have long had a habit of dropping certain consonants out of their dialect and using in their place a glottal stop—a pause or click—instead. That *k* which has been dropped out of Havaiki, for instance, has always been a great favorite of the Hawaiian and of the New Zealand Maori. A notable drop-out in our islands is the *ng* of, for example, Tonga and Samoa. An illustration of this is "Raiatea" itself, which would be spelled by a purist, Ra'iatea. In other dialects it would be Rangiatea, "Rangi" meaning the sky, or heaven as we would translate it, and "atea" meaning wide space, the whole, as Teuira Henry puts it, meaning "Expansive Sky." Since this glottal stop is confusing to the uninitiated, it has been disregarded in this book, except in the first instance of its use when it will be indicated by the conventional introverted apostrophe (or hamzah) and put in quotation marks. Thereafter the hamzah will be omitted. Variations in the island dialects which will be taken for granted in this script are the well-known interchangeables: *r* for *l*, *h* for *f*, *k* for *t*, etc. I believe that these were all originally much more consistent than they are today. Many of the differences must have sprung from long separations of distance and time, but it seems to me that most of them came from the ears of missionaries endeavoring to translate the sounds into written letters. We all know the nursery tongue-twister "round the rugged rocks," etc. In early accounts of Hawaii we read of "Tamehameha" and "Honoruru." Amongst early accounts of Raiatea, Beaglehole notes in Cook's

Journal, "On board the *Endeavour* we have for instance, Uliatoah, Uliateir, Olyatea, Ulatea, Ulieteah, to take only one island, where all the English ears heard an *l*. Parkinson's version, Yoolee-Eteah, is useful, for it shows us that the name thus picked up for Raiatea was the older one given by Ellis as Ioretea; Parkinson's 'Yoo' and the English 'U' of the other versions representing the rapidly-sounded *Io*-. Ioretea may represent *Uriatea*."

When I write of the very distinctive culture of the Polynesians, just what is meant? The character of a culture is not easy to analyze or describe systematically and yet it is easy to recognize, to feel, and to sense. I know of no universal balance sheet or tabulation whereby the varying cultures of the world can be compared. This is a job for the sociologists, but I have not been able to find any professional set of rules for classification. I'm not sure it is possible to draw one up that would have much value, any more than it is fruitful to compare the music of Mozart with that of Wagner, a Van Gogh with an El Greco, Shakespeare with Dante. Yet their differences and distinctions are almost glaringly recognizable.

I think it was Victor Heiser who once told of a fascinating experiment he and some of his students or colleagues had conducted. They wanted to explore the possible effects of diet on character. They took a big batch of laboratory rats, all of them with the same genetic background, and divided them into three lots. To one lot they fed a typical English diet: tea, roast beef, fish and chips, vegetable marrow, brussel sprouts, puddings, milk, whiskey, etc. A second received French fare: wine, coffee, snails bourguignonne, poulet marengo, bouillabaisse, bread, peche melba, pressed duck, crepes suzettes, a bit of absinthe. The third of course got a spread of German sauerkraut, beer, wiener schnitzel, pigs feet, dumplings, pumpernickel, liederkranz, more beer, liverwurst, apple strüdle. This went on over a couple of years, many generations, and sure enough the distinctive national traits emerged: superior superiority, amorous superiority, blitzkrieg superiority. Then the rats were all mixed together again and given the standard laboratory feeding. Sure enough again, they returned in a few generations to their original universal, ratty character. The scientists were delighted, but they agreed, chuckling, that they did not know just what they had proved.

So we might start with the Polynesians' diet, probably more simple, monotonous, and bland than you will find anywhere else in the world. And yet they are generally conceded to be the handsomest physical specimens of humanity that we have so far evolved. What have they done with their gorgeous bodies? They laze and sleep more than any man. They love better, play better, and (in intermittent, volatile spurts) work (or at least expend energy) better than other cultures. All this seems, however, to contradict rather than derive from a diet conditioning; perhaps it is a diet rebellion. Douglas Oliver acutely observes, "To begin with, it seems quite incontrovertible that eating was regarded . . . as one of the supreme pleasures of life—and not just as a means of restoring energy or of warding off illness and assuaging the discomfort of hunger, but as a recurrent end in itself."

But let us not get bogged down in the causes of such things. There may be many more: sunshine, water aplenty, sweet-scented flowers galore, bread (fruit) aplenty with nary a sweat from the brow, watery wastes of insulation from the rest of the madding world . . . . Let us look at results. You have learned in reading this book something of the Religion of the Polynesian and religion, I suppose, is the primary individualistic creation of any culture. His Morals—sexual, social, personal—have been sketched in. His Economics (virtually nonexistent in our contexts), his Warfare (highly conventionalized—he knew well the bow and arrow but never used them to wound or kill a man), his Mythology, Folklore and Geneologies, Amusements, Ceremony (including kava drinking), Arts (including tatu, whose universal name "tattoo" is Polynesian and which attained a stature of fine art only in his islands), Domestic Life including tapa or bark cloth dress, Seafaring, etc. etc. have all been described by many other writers (including myself) elsewhere. They are all distinctive and individualistic . . . and fascinating, but they are subjects that are much too complex and detailed to suffer by repetition or summary here. The best descriptive analysis is that of Douglas Oliver in his recent monumental three-volume study, ANCIENT TAHITIAN SOCIETY. He addresses himself specifically to our particular islanders, whom he calls *Maohis*, differentiating them even from the Tuamotuans and Marquesans. I don't like his terminology because I think it is merely another variant on Maori and I don't believe they were as segregated from their neighbors as he does. But his scholarly gleanings from the "sources," or earliest European reports, are as definitive as any are ever likely to be.

What I would like to do is call attention to a few random traits or habits that I have noticed in the daily life of the people of the central Polynesian islands that are peculiar to them, that would identify them immediately as Polynesian and only Polynesian, even if you were observing them from a distance in an auditorium or agora, or athletic field or fairgrounds intermingled with many other peoples of many other races and nationalities. First off in acknowledging a greeting they always raise their heads (or chins): they never nod or bow as we of America, Europe and Asia do. When a mother signals a child to come to her (or a man to a friend or servant or wife) the motion of the beckoning hand is always downward, not upward as is ours. Conversely to motion one to go away or indicate that someone has departed this way or that, the hand starts downward and flips up. When a man gestures to show you directions along a winding path, up trails in the hills, a course through a pass or channel or to a distant harbor, his hand is outstretched with fingers together as he weaves his directions in the air. He never points with the index finger as we do. A "yes" or agreement or "I understand" without words (and it almost always is wordless) is a raising of the eyebrows, only that, except occasionally a low-intoned "E" (ay) meaning merely that "I hear you." When a man shows you the length of a fish he caught or any other lineal measurement under a yard, he extends his right arm downward, fingers closed, palm toward you and marks the measure with his left hand, fingers closed, palm upward at a right angle to his right arm on his palm, forearm, upper arm. He never spreads his two hands or fingers apart as we do to indicate length. His eyes flash like lightening strokes when he speaks animatedly (as he so often does) as do Italians, but he does not gesture much with his hands, nor does he purse and wriggle his lips à la francais. When you bring a Polynesian a gift (for a birthday, an anniversary, an engraved silver cup for a new-born, a Christmas present) he has a curious and invariable and (to a European) disconcerting habit of taking it without so much as a smile, never even a nod of thanks, never even unwrapping it in your presence, but spiriting it away to the recesses of his house. And nothing is ever told you about it forever after, even though you know he is deeply grateful and painfully appreciative.

Well so it goes. Strange little idiosyncracies of behavior and custom passed down to them through the centuries; no reasons for them, no sense in them; they are just Polynesian and after two centuries of intense exposure to and domination by European culture, they persist as blithely and unconcernedly as does his native language with its glottal stops in spite of foreign language schools and churches, as do his ways and freedoms of making love in spite of his masters' missionaries and mores.

SYDNEY PARKINSON

2. Parkinson's Plants

For the amateur interested in the flowers and food plants that were such an intimate part of the Raiatean's everyday life before the white man came, and so revealing of his symbiosis, physical and psychic, with his flora, Sydney Parkinson's list is the best one I know. It is reproduced here just as he wrote it except that his long *s* (*ſ*) has been converted to our conventional *s* and his lengthy comments on two plants, the breadfruit and coconut, have been cut to their first sentences because enough has already been written about them in the text. Douglas Oliver estimates that only about 10% of these plants were truly indigenous: that is, present when the Polynesian arrived. He introduced the rest and, much later on, the European brought a cascade of new ones from all over the world. So this list is almost lost in the flora you will find today.

Parkinson's comments or descriptions are well worth a careful reading because they show not only the ingenuity of the Raiateans in the use of their flora, but also the keen and painstaking perception of Sydney Parkinson.

PLANTS of Use for Food, Medicine, &c. in Otaheite

Native Name — Latin Name

Teatea-maowa. — *Jasminum-didymum.*

Grows upon the hills; has a very sweet-smelling white flower, which the natives admire much.

E ava. — *Piper-inebrians.*

The expressed juice of this plant they drink to intoxicate themselves. [Illustration page 178].

E to. — *Saccharum-dulcis.*

Of this cane they make no sugar, but content themselves with sucking the juice out of it.

E mohoo. — *Cyperus-alatus.*

The stalks of this plant, stripped of their pulp, which they perform with a sharp shell, make a sort of thread used for several common purposes.

Sydney Parkinson is, to me, one of the most engaging personalities in that very colorful company of Cook's first voyage. He was the son of a brewer in Edinburgh who was a Quaker "well-known and esteemed by all ranks of men," to quote Sydney's brother Stanfield. But alas he was "remiss in prosecuting the recovery of his just debts" and left his wife, the two boys, and their sister Brittania destitute. Sydney was to be a woollen draper, but he took to painting flowers and showed such a flair that when he went to London shortly after his father's death, he was quickly taken up by eminent botanists. Naturally enough they soon introduced him to Joseph Banks, Esq., and forthwith he was signed on, as one of two botanical draughtsmen, for the great voyage to the South Seas . . . at a yearly salary of £ 80.

When his fellow artist died not long after they rounded the Horn, Parkinson took over the whole task of recording graphically not only the botany, but birds, marine life, Polynesian life and whatever else Banks required of him.

But he sketched for himself as well and his output was prodigious even though, it was said, swarms of flies settled on him and on his colours as he drew and painted in the Tahitian islands. His work, as you can see in this book, also had verve and intelligence. He was generally a favorite aboard ship, much admired for his modesty as well as his industry according to reports by his shipmates.

A glimpse of him at work is given us by Banks later on as they were coasting Australia. "This evening we finished drawing the plants got in the last

Jasminum didymum.

Taihinnoo *Tournefortia-serica.*
E tow. *Cordia-sebestena.*

The leaves of these two plants are ingredients in their red dye, or matee, for their cloth.

E marra. *Nauclea-orientalis.*

Of the timber of this tree they build their large canoes. [As stated on page 131, mara was a favorite in addition to Beaglehole's three, page 141.]

E teea-ree. *Gardenia-florida.*

This was originally brought from some other island to Otaheite, and there planted on account of its most fragrant flower, which they crop as soon as grown and stick in their ears, calling it E teea-ree, that is, the flower, by way of eminence. [Illustration page 23]

Taowdeehaow. *Convolvulus-alatus.*

The stalks of this plant they give young children to suck.

E oomarra. *Convolvulus-chrysorizus.*

Planted and cultivated by the natives, on account of its root, which is the sweet potatoe of the South-sea Islands. [*Ipomea batatas*, illustration page 104].

Pohooe. *Convolvulus-Brasiliensis.*

Of this plant they make a sort of seine, which they use in such ground where they cannot use another.

E maireeo. *Galaxa-oppositi-folia.*

The leaf of this plant is one of the ingredients in their manoe. [Monoi is their ubiquitous massage cream. Its base is coconut oil and it is perfumed with tiare tahiti, sandalwood, jasmin or other scents.]

E deva, or E reva. *Galaxa-sparsa.*

This plant has a pretty large white flower like that of an oleander. Of the wood of this tree they make their pahaoos, or drums.

E booa, or E pooa. *Solanum-latifolium.*

The leaves of this plant they use in making their red dye or mattee.

harbour, which had been kept fresh till this time by means of tin boxes and wet cloths. In 14 days just, our draughtsman has made 94 sketch drawings, so quick a hand has he acquired by use."

But, homeward bound less than a year later, when they were only eleven days out from Java Head, Parkinson died suddenly in the dreadful epidemic that Cook called "the Fevers and fluxes" which took 23 of the ship's company in six weeks.

The sequel to his tale was a sad one, a bitter and tragic confrontation between his brother Stanfield and Banks over Sydney's writings, pictures, artifacts, and nature collections. His famous *Journal* is scrappy, although he had a talent for words as well as brush and pen. On first sight of Tahiti he sees its landscape "uneven as a piece of crumpled paper . . . mountains piled on mountains to an amazing height." His actual manuscript was purportedly lost and only notes for it survived, but much of it is lively and perceptive as these comments on "Plants" right clearly show. What an artist we might have known, had he not died so young.

Pouraheitee. *Solanum-viride.*

The leaves of this plant, baked, are eaten as greens.

E nono. *Morinda-citri-folia.*

The root of this tree they use to dye their garments yellow, and eat the fruit of it.

b. Morinda citrifolia Nono

E tee. *Draccana-terminalis.*

Of this plant there are five different sorts, yielding a large root, which is eaten, and counted very good food, by the islanders of the South-seas.

Tootaoopa. *Loranthus-stelis.*

This plant is remarkable for nothing except its name, which signifies the Oopa, or pigeons dung; that bird feeds on the berries, and voids the stones on the trunk of trees, where it grows.

E peea. *Chaitea-tacca.*

The root of this plant, properly prepared, makes an excellent strong jelly, like to blanc-mange, of the nature of salop, for which it is very justly admired by these islanders.

Tawhannoo. *Guettarda-speciosa.*

The timber of this tree, which grows pretty large at Toopbai, and other low islands near Otaheite, serves to make stools, chests, paste-troughs, and various other utensils; they also build canoes of it.

E awaow. *Daphne-capitata.*

This plant is used to poison fish, in order to catch them; and, for this purpose, they beat or mash it together and throw it into the rivers and sea within the reefs.

E owhe. *Arundo-bambos.*

This is the common bamboe of which these islanders make great use; the large joints they keep to hold water and oil; of the small they make arrows, flutes, cases to hold small things; and, when cut into slips, they serve them for knives, and cut tolerably well.

E motoo. *Melastoma-malabathrica.*

This plant is one of those which they hang up upon their whatta-note-toobapaow, or burial-stand, to be eaten by the soul of the deceased. [Illustration page 94]

E hee; or E ratta. *Aniotum-fagiferum.*

This is a tall and stately tree which bears a round flat fruit, covered with a thick tough coat, and, when roasted and stripped of its rind, eats as well as a chesnut. [Maape; illustration of tree page 27; illustration of roasted nuts page 175]

E avee. *Spondias-dulcis.*

This is a large stately tree, and often grows to the height of forty and fifty feet: the fruit, which, I believe, is peculiar to these isles, is of an oval shape, yellow when ripe, and grows in bunches of three or four, and is about the size of a middling apple, with a large stringy core: it is a very wholesome and palatable fruit, improving on the taste, which is nearest that of a mangoe; it is strongly impregnated with turpentine, and makes excellent pies when green. The wood serves for building canoes, and for several other purposes.

Pouraoo, *Crataeva-frondosa.*
and epooataroorroo.

The fruit of this shrub they lay upon their corpses, and hang it upon their burial whattas, it having an agreeable bitter smell: it is one of those which are sacred to their god Tane, and, for that reason, is generally planted in, or by the small Morais, and nead their houses, called Morai Roma Tane, which are a sort of altar near the houses, upon which they offer victuals.

E peereepeeree. *Euphorbia-develata.*

This plant is full of a milky juice, with which they dye their garments of an indifferent brown colour.

E aowiree. *Terminalia-glabrata.*

This tree, which grows to a large size, is often planted in their Morais, and near their houses, for the sake of its agreeable shade; the wood serves to build canoes, make chests, stools and drums: the kernel of the nut which is in the fruit, though small, has a very pleasant taste.

Spondias dulcis.
Sydney Parkinson pinx 1769.

E ratta, or e pooratta. *Metrosideros-spectabilis.*

This tree, or shrub, grows upon the Tooaroa, or Lower-hills, and is much resorted to by the venee, or small blue parrot, which feeds upon the flowers, and is often caught here, by means of a glewy juice which issues out from the tops of the stalks, when broke by their feeding upon them, and catches them like bird-lime: the flowers are full of beautiful scarlet stamina; the natives stick them in their ears by way of ornament; and the leaves are put in their monoe, when they can get nothing sweeter.

E arrarooa. *Psidium-myrtifolium.*

The only use they make of this tree, which has a flower like a myrtle, is to make their totos or clubs and ewha's, or a sort of lances, being very tough; they call it an eraow paree, or the cunning tree.

E heiya. *Eugenia-mallaccensis.*

This tree grows upon the lower-hills, having great clusters of crimson flowers, full of stamina of the same colour, much like an almond-blossom, but more brilliant: the fruit, when ripe, is red, and as big as one's fist; sweet, very agreeable to the palate, and full of seeds: it is very well known in the East-India islands, where it is esteemed delicious fruit.

Tamanno. *Calophyllum-inophyllum.*

This is a most beautiful verdant tree, that grows to a large size, bearing spikes of white flowers: with the juice of the fruit and leaves they dye their garments a pale yellow, which, at the same time, gives them a rich perfume. The wood is greatly valued by them on account of its beauty and duration. They build canoes, make stools, and other utensils of it: it is most likely planted in the Morais, being sacred to their god Tane. [Illustration page 157].

E poo-aiho. *Saccharum-fatuum.*

With bundles of this grass, lit up, they allure the fish to the edges of the reefs, carrying them in their hands at night.

E atoorree. *Portulacca-lutea.*

This sort of purslain grows very common in the low islands, where the inhabitants bake and eat it, and account it very good food.

E hootoo. *Betonica-splendida.*

This beautiful tree grows to a considerable height, and bears a very large and specious white flower, full of long purple stamina, with which they sometimes deck their heads, and sometimes stick them in their ears: the fruit, powdered, they throw into the water to kill fish; and of the wood they build small canoes. [Illustration page 140].

E pooamattapeepee. *Besleria-laurifolia.*

The flower of this tree is much admired on account of its sweet scent, for which reason they stick them in their ears and hair, and put them among their garments, and into their monoe. The wood is very tough and lasting, and of it they make drums, and thwarts across their canoes.

E neearohettee. *Stachys-dentata, or ruellia-fragrans.*

The juice of this plant, mixed with several others, they use as a plaister to cure any sort of wounds.

E noonanoona. *Boerhavia-procumbens.*

The stalks of this plant are eaten when they have no better food.

E ava-vaidai *Piper-latifolium.*

The juice of this plant has not the intoxicating quality of the other, so that they prudently make an offering of it to their Eatooas, on whose altars they hang bunches of it.

E pooraow. *Hibiscus-cuspidatus.*

The bark of this tree yields an excellent stuff for making all sorts of twine, cord, and ropes. Of the wood they make their bows, beams and pillars of their houses, small canoes, stools, and various other utensils. Of the bark of the plant, when young, they weave a sort of matting, which is very neat, and is called by the same name as the tree. The wood that remains after the bark is taken off, being very light, serves, instead of cork, to float their seins, and for handles to their fisgigs; and to rub together to get fire.

E pooraow-toro-ceree. *Hibiscus-tricuspis.*

This plant is pretty much like the last, and is used for the same purposes, but is inferior in quality.

Hibiscus. Abelmoschus.

E aiowe. *Hibiscus-rosa-sinensis.*

This tree is admired on account of its beautiful scarlet flower, of which the young people make garlands for their hair, stick them in their ears, and rub their lances with them to make them look red. [Illustration page 154].

E wawei. *Gossipium-religiosum.*

This is a species of cotton of which they have not yet found out the use.

E meerro. *Thespesia-populnea.*

This beautiful tree is planted in all Morais, being held sacred to Tane: they also make use of it as an emblem of peace; and always bring it in their hands when they meet with strange people. It yields a middling sort of timber, and is made use of for several purposes.

E peereeperee. *Urena-lobata.*

The seeds of this plant are of the nature of a burr, from whence its name, to glue or stick to any thing. The boys play the same tricks with it as the children in Europe with the burr. They also make maro's, or a sort of mat of the bark.

Berdeebeedeeo. *Abrus-pricatorius.*

The seed of this plant is the well-known Indian pea with a black spot: of these they form ear-rings, and also stick them on a fillet which they wear on their head.

E atai, erythoina. *Corallodendron.*

This is a large tree, and remarkable for its bright scarlet flower, making a most beautiful show. The venee feeds upon its flowers, and is caught with the clammy juice that issues out of it; the women make garlands of them, and put them round their heads.

E owhaee. *Aeschynomene-speciosa.*

This shrub grows wild, in great abundance on the island of Toopbai; and is planted on the other islands to shade their houses; and the flower of it, which is very beautiful, they often stick in their ears.

E hora. *Galega-piscatoria.*

With this plant, beaten small, they poison or stupify fish, throwing it into the water, by which means they are caught.

E peepee. *Phaseolus-amoenus.*

The stalks of this plant make a very good thread for weaving nets and seins. Of the flowers, which are very pretty, they make garlands for their heads.

E vaeenoo. *Cotula-bicolor.*
E tooho. *Epipactis-purpurea.*

Both these plants, bruised, are ingredients in their Erapaow-mai, or plaister to cure sores.

Taro. *Arum-esculentum.*

The roots of this plant, of which there are several varieties, are as good as Ignames, and are reckoned very wholesome common food in the South-sea islands. The leaves, when baked, taste as well as greens.

E ape. *Arum-costatum.*

The root of this plant is as good as the last, but considerably larger: the leaves, which are very smooth and extremely large, are used to wrap up, or lay any sort of victuals upon.

E toa-casuarina. *Equisetifolia.*

This is one of the best woods they have; it is very hard and heavy, and coloured like mahogany. They make their clubs, lances, cloth-beaters, and several other knick-nacks and utensils of it.

Tooneenna. *Hernandia-ovigera.*

Of the wood of this tree they make a sort of very small canoes, and several other necessary utensils.

E hooe-rorro. *Cucurbita-puriens.*

The fruit of this tree is about the size of a small orange, very hard, and quite round, serving them, instead of bottles, to put their monoe or oil in.

Moemoe. *Phyllanthus-anceps.*

The only remarkable thing about this plant is the leaves, which shut up at night, from whence its name, which signifies sleepy.

E aowte. *Morus-papyriferus.*

This is the shrub from which they make their finest and most beautiful cloth; (tapa) and is probably the same with that of which they make paper in China. They never let it grow old, but cut it down when it is about a man's height, stripping the bark off, and laying it to soak in water. Of this they make their cloth either thick or thin as they please. They plant it in beds, and take great pains in the cultivation of it.

E ora. *Uritica-argentea, or Urtica-candicans.*

Of the stalks of this nettle, beaten out, they make their best lines for their fishhooks, which has the quality of not rotting with salt-water; they also make their belts or girdles of it, but very seldom garments; their best seins are also made of it.

E tootooe. *Telopaea-perspicua.*

Of the bark of this tree, soaked in water, they make that gummy substance which they put upon their dark-coloured cloth to make it glossy, and keep out the rain. The fruit of this tree is a sort of nut, which yields a very fat kernel, of which they make their black dye, used in Tataowing, by burning them and receiving the smoke. Strung upon a reed or stick they serve instead of candles, and give a very good light.

E ooroo. *Sitodium-altile.*

This tree, which yields the bread-fruit so often mentioned by the voyagers to the South-seas, may justly be stiled the Staff-of-life to these islanders, for from it they draw most of their support. [Illustration page 115]

E awharra. *Pandanus-tectorius.*

This tree generally grows on the sandy hillocks by the sea-side, and is found in great plenty on all the low islands; the leaves are long, like those of sedge, sawed on the edge; the flowers are male and female, growing upon different trees; those of the male-flower smell very sweet; and, of the bractea of them, which are white, they make a sort of garlands to put round their heads; the fruit is orange-colour, and as big as one's head, consisting of a congeries of small cones, like those of the Anana, or Pine-apple, which they much resemble: the bottom of these cones, sucked when full ripe, yield a flat insipid sweetness, and are eaten by the children; but the chief use of this tree is in the leaves, which, when plucked and dried, make excellent thatching for their houses, and various sorts of mats and baskets. This is the Palmetto of the eastern voyagers. [Fara, illustration page 33]

E mattee. *Ficus-tinctoria.*

The figs of this tree are one of the chief ingredients in their red-dye for their garments: when they use them they nip or bite off the stalk close to the fruit, at which time a small drop of milky juice issues out; this they either shake upon the tow-leaves, used in this dye, or else into a cocoa-nut shell, with a little water, or cocoa-nut milk; and then dip the leaves into it, which they roll up in a small bundle, and work or squeeze them between the palm and their fingers, till the red colour is produced by the mixture of the two juices; but what is very odd, these leaves being beaten in a mortar, and the juice taken from them and mixed with the fig-milk, will not produce the same colour. Of the bark of this tree very good twine is made, which is of particular use for making of seins, and other nets.

E aowa. *Ficus-prolixa.*

This tree is remarkable on account of its trunk, which grows to an enormous size, by the branches hanging down, and taking root again, which makes a very grotesque figure. Of the bark of young plants, raised on purpose, they make a sort of cloth, naturally of a russet-hue, which they call Ora, being worn in the mornings, and much valued by them, especially that which is beaten very fine and thin. [Banyan, illustration page 105]

E toee. *Zezyphoides-argentea.*

The wood of this tree they make use of for various purposes, such as sterns of canoes, heightening boards for ditto, and beams to beat their cloth upon.

E apeeree. *Dodonaea-viscosa.*

The wood of this tree, which is very tough, serves to make a particular sort of weapon, which they carry in their hand when they dive after sharks, and other large fish.

E tive. *Dracontium-polyphyllum.*

The root of this is used to make a jelly like the Peea, but is not near so good.

Meiya. *Musa-paradisaico.*

This is the well known tropical fruit called Plaintains, and Bananas, of which there is a great variety in these islands: they reckon more than twenty sorts which differ in shape and taste; some of these are for eating raw, and others best boiled, and will serve instead of bread: they plant them in a rich soil, and take great pains in their cultivation.

Faihe. *Musa-bihai.*

This is another sort of Plaintains, which generally grow wild

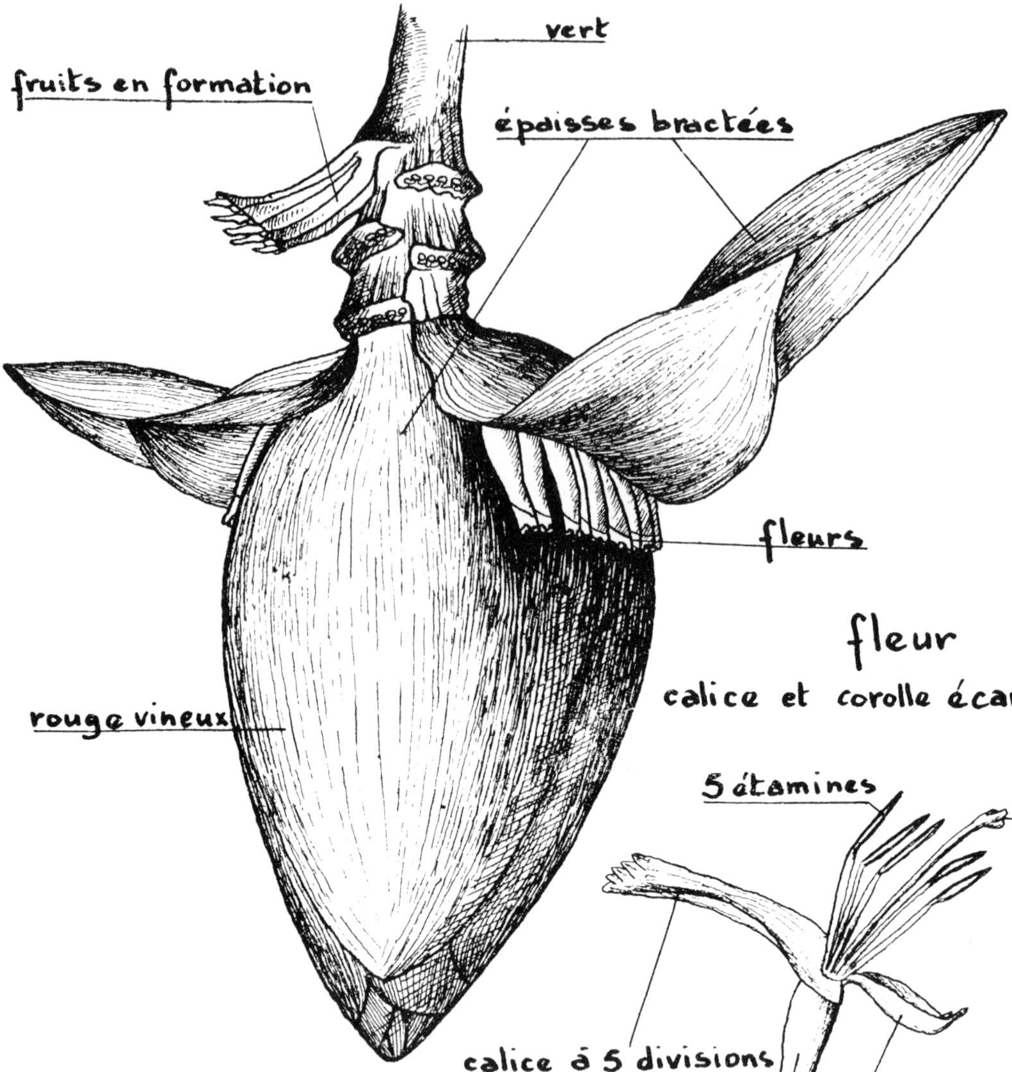

fleur

calice et corolle écartés

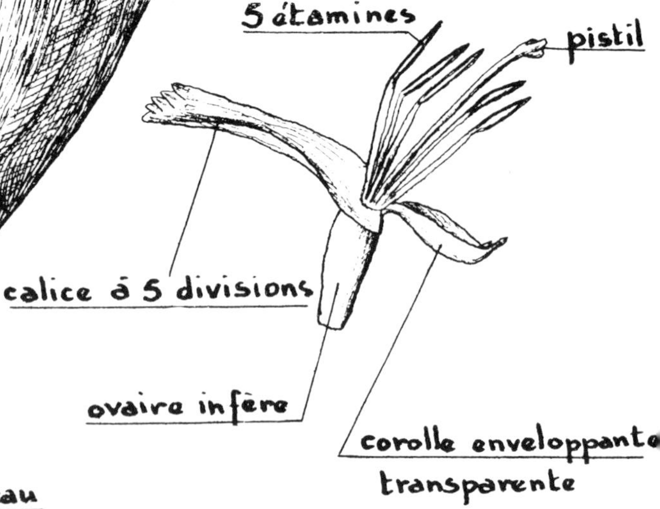

coupe d'une banane

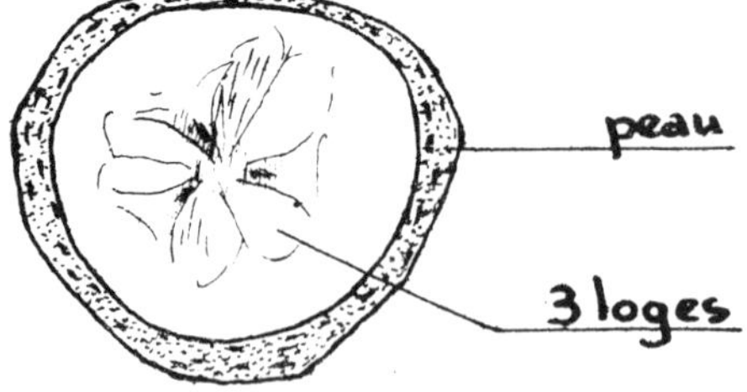

in the mountains, and sometimes are planted by them; they are far inferior to the last, have a considerable astringency, and eat best boiled or roasted. There are four different sorts, and the leaves of this and the last, serve to put victuals upon; and the rind of the trunk to make a sort of baskets called Papa-meiya. [Illustration page 17]

E aree. *Coccus-nucifer.*

This palm, the fruit of which is so well known in all places within the tropics, seems to be a native of these islands, being found every where in the greatest plenty, and in the greatest perfection, especially on the two low islands, called by them Motoos. [Coconut illustrations sprinkled throughout.]

E papa.

Of the leaves of this tree, which are very white and glistering when dried, they make their evanne-matting, much admired for its beauty.

E howira.

This grows chiefly in the low islands; of the split leaves they make their best mats for garments, to sit, and sleep upon.

E yeiyei.

This plant is of the nature of osier; of the stalks of it they work their round baskets, which they call Heenei, and in which they keep their victuals, and all their utensils.

Doodooe-awai & Oheparra.

With these they dye their poowhirre, or brown cloth.

Patarra.

An eatable root, which I did not see.

E nioee.

A fine eatable fruit, of a red color, which I did not see.

E apatahei.

An elegant flower, which I also did not see. [!]

Oowhe note Maowa. *Dioscorea-alata.*

This plant produces the root so well known by the name of Ignames, all over the East and West-Indies: they have several sorts of it, but that which grows upon the hills is the best.

E nahae.

This is a fern, which has an extraordinary sweet-smell, and, for this reason it is used by the better sort of people to sleep on.

E ahei.

The wood of this tree, has a very rich and delicious smell; is of a yellow colour, and is the principal ingredient used in perfuming their monoe, being grated small, and put to soak amongst it; as it is very scarce, it is in great request amongst them; we could never get a sight of the tree, but were told it grew on the mountains. They have various other vegetables with which they perfume their monoe, and likewise their cloaths, the names of these are, Pooeva, Maiteeraow, Annee, Noonna, Ehaee, Amea, and Matehooa. [Sandalwood we call it.]

E atoo.

A plant of which they make mat garments.

And the idols he shall utterly abolish.—*Isaiah* ii. 18. (See page 116.)

3. European Impacts

It is interesting to compare attitudes and objectives of the various Europeans who infiltrated the vast Pacific. First were the Spaniards looking for gold, who, when it became apparent that there was none, shot the natives for sport. The Dutch, looking for trade and finding none, ignored them. The English explorers are best characterized perhaps by the instructions given to Captain Cook by the Admiralty.

"To exercise the utmost patience and forebearance with respect to the Natives of the several Lands where the Ship may touch. To check the petulance of the Sailors, and restrain the wanton use of Fire Arms. To have it still in view that sheding the blood of those people is a crime of the highest nature . . . . They are natural, and in the strictest sense of the word, the legal possessors of the several Regions they inhabit . . . . They may naturally and justly attempt to repell intruders, whom they may apprehend are come to disturb them in the quiet possession of their country, whether that apprehension be well or ill founded. There fore every effort should be made to avoid violence: if it became inevitable, then the Natives when brought under should be treated with distinguished humanity, and made sensible that the Crew still considers them as Lords of the Country."

The French, bemused by Rousseau, became ecstatically romantic in the wake of Bougainville and his "Nouvelle Cythere," later on determinedly and militarily acquisitive. Their missionaries had the bad luck to be preceded by the London Protestants and to this day are very much in the minority. They did, however, gain ascendency in the Marquesas. Those fierce islanders discouraged the early Protestants by eating them so that the Catholics had a clear field once the warriors were subdued by French canon.

The English missionaries, Protestants all, set out with fiery zeal, charged with the fervor of the Directors of the London Missionary Society. "Evangelical truths are the weapons of your warfare, let them not be covered with unsightly rust, nor blunted by too much polish—mind chiefly the *edge*. Remember also, that the word is a *two-edged* sword, the law and the gospel—the one to strike conviction into the conscience of sinners; and the other, to cut off sin from the believer in Jesus, as well as to lop off and consign to destruction all apostates . . . let the poor ignorant natives *take knowledge* of you . . . But are you not going to Otaheite? for the sake of returning to which island of sensual delights a ship's crew mutinied? Ah, remember the history of the antediluvian church; ye "sons of God," beware of the "daughters of men." . . . above all, when they [the Missionaries] survey the hundreds of millions of souls lying in the darkness of heathenism . . . how ought every Missionary to weep and make supplication, wrestling with the Great Angel of the Covenant, that he may be kept pure from the blood of all men, and may gain the prize of turning many to righteousness . . . .

In all attempts to convince the natives of their crimes, we should particularly select those instances of depravity which are most frequently striking, viz, the shocking crime of shedding human blood; the horrid murder of children; the abominable public prostitutions, and such enormities as carry upon the face of them something revolting even to humanity. . . ."

But that zeal was tempered. "The Missionaries must make the natives sensible, that in settling among them they have no unreasonable demands to make, no claims of ambition, arrogance, or avarice; that they are disposed to acknowledge with the purest integrity and respect, the dominion of the natives over their own island, and all its productions."

The traders who came next were as we all know a mixed bag of good and evil, mostly evil. Of the tourists . . . we shall see. The prognosis is not encouraging, but the Polynesian is still polynesian and perhaps, just perhaps, growing more so as the generations pass.

Credits

Paintings, drawings, photographs, etc. which illustrate this book are identified here and referred to by the numbers of the page on which they appear. In each case when the source is mentioned, grateful acknowledgement for permission to use the illustration is implicit. When the British Museum and British Library are referred to, my intention is to acknowledge the further consent of the Trustees of the British Museum and the Library Board of the British Library.

Permission to quote rather extensively from the footnotes of J. C. Beaglehole in THE ENDEAVOUR JOURNAL OF JOSEPH BANKS was kindly granted by the Trustees of the Public Library of New South Wales, publishers in association with Angus and Robertson.

2–3. Elevation of Raiatea; painting by Henry Roberts, photo Mitchell Library, Sydney.
5. Apetahi medallion, photo Michel Liaut
8. Opoa, drawing Jacques Boullaire
11a. Schooner *Chance*, photo Alexander C. Brown
11b. Turia, photo Alexander C. Brown
12. Fetuna 1929, photo Alexander C. Brown
13. Nao Nao and Fetuna pass, photo K. P. Emory
15a. Farika, photo Axel Poignant
15b. Turo, photo Yosi Sinoto
16. Fetuna house, photo K. P. Emory
17. Narii, photo Axel Poignant
18. Oropiro by day, photo K. P. Emory
19a. Oropiro by night, photo K. P. Emory
19b. Coco sprout, drawing Jacques Boullaire
20. Tiare apetahi in situ, photo Axel Poignant
23. Tiare tahiti, painting S. Parkinson, British Museum (Natural History)
25. *Apetahia raiatensis, H. Bn.* drawing Drake del Castillo, photo New York Botanical Gardens Library
26. Conch, D'Urville *Atlas, Voyage de l'Astrolabe*, photo Albert Oglesby
27. Maape grove, photo Bishop Museum
29. Temehani ridges, photo Bishop Museum
30. Golden Plover, photo Bishop Museum
31. Tiare apetahi bush, drawing Robert MacLean

Color Section

Following page 88

Appendix

Index

An asterisk * indicates that the subject occurs throughout or so frequently that a list of page references seems superfluous in a text as short as this. In these cases, where appropriate, only the first or key definitional reference is given.